FINANCIAL TRAUMA

Why Money Isn't Just About Money

FINANCIAL TRAUMA

Why Money Isn't Just About Money

WENDY MOLYNEUX

Disclaimer: The information in this book is for educational purposes only and is not intended as financial, legal, medical, or mental health advice. It should not substitute for professional guidance tailored to your individual circumstances. All matters regarding your health or finances require professional guidance. Please consult qualified professionals before making financial decisions or addressing mental or physical health concerns.

All names and identifying characteristics have been changed to protect the privacy of the individuals involved.

The author and publisher make no guarantees regarding specific outcomes and assume no liability for any inaccuracies, losses, damages, or distress that may result from the use of this information. Readers use this content at their own discretion and risk.

ISBN: 978-0972174213 (Print)
978-0972174206 (eBook)

Library of Congress Suggested Cataloging-in-Publication Data

Molyneux, Wendy

Financial Trauma: Why Money Isn't Just About Money

1. Finance, Personal—Psychological aspects
2. Money—Psychological aspects
3. Wealth—Psychological aspects

332.02401019—dc23

Published in the United States by Glyph River

Author's Note

I approach this work as both a professional and someone with lived experience of financial trauma. My perspective is inevitably shaped by my own journey and context, including experiences that have afforded me certain privileges while also creating vulnerabilities. While the internal processes I describe affect us all, I recognize that systemic forces create different pathways to financial trauma for different communities. Throughout this book, I've aimed to honor both the universal patterns and the particular contexts that shape how financial trauma manifests.

To

David and Seth

Table of Contents

1

Understanding Financial Trauma

You've probably been told your money problems can be solved with a budget. Or a spreadsheet. Or a little more willpower. But what if the real problem isn't the numbers? What if it's the memories, the shame, the fear that still lives in your nervous system?

Money decisions touch every part of life, yet most financial advice skips over this deeper layer. When someone overspends, avoids financial tasks, or feels emotionally flooded around money, the root cause often traces back to experiences that shaped their relationship with money, experiences that were traumatic.

What You'll Learn in This Chapter

- Why financial trauma deserves its own definition
- How traumatic experiences, both chronic and acute, shape your relationship with money
- What this book will cover, who it's for, and how it can support you

What Is Financial Trauma?

Financial trauma refers to the responses that arise from experiences which threaten a person's financial security, stability, or overall well-being.

When trauma intersects with money, the consequences ripple across life because finances intertwine with every other area of living.

To understand money trauma, we need to understand trauma itself, not just as a concept, but as a lived experience with lasting imprints.

While many definitions exist, I've chosen one that's especially inclusive and widely recognized by trauma professionals. It comes from SAMHSA, the U.S. Substance Abuse and Mental Health Services Administration:[1]

> *Trauma results from an event, series of events, or a set of circumstances an individual experiences as physically or emotionally harmful or threatening, which may have lasting adverse effects on the individual's functioning and mental, physical, social, emotional, or spiritual well-being. Traumatic events may be experienced by an individual, a generation, or an entire community or culture.*

In the end, trauma is a *wound*, the word's original meaning in Greek. Not all wounds are visible. Some heal on their own. Others linger, shape us, and follow us through life, even when we can't name them.

It's crucial to keep in mind that people react to similar events differently. Many people who go through a potentially traumatic experience don't become psychologically traumatized. They may feel significant distress or a sense of overwhelm at the time, but their capacity to cope remains intact.

Others, after exposure to the same event, may develop post-traumatic stress disorder (PTSD) or other trauma responses that reshape how their nervous system reacts to certain situations.

This variation matters. Your response to financial difficulties is uniquely yours, and there's no right or wrong way to be affected by challenging experiences.

One of the most powerful descriptions of trauma comes from Dr. Gabor Maté, who said:[2]

> *Trauma is not what happens to you; it is what happens inside you as a result of what happens to you... It is not the blow on the head, but the concussion I get.*

It's not the job you lost. Or the debt you racked up. Or the house you couldn't hold onto.

It's about what happened inside you as a result.

That's where the real work begins.

This inner impact, what happens inside you, is what distinguishes trauma from other difficult life experiences.

And here's something important: Trauma isn't always a medical label. Sometimes, it's simply the weight you've been carrying: the panic, the shame, the stuckness you can't shake.

While this book doesn't focus on diagnosis of conditions like PTSD or Complex PTSD, it's helpful to know not all trauma meets the criteria for a clinical diagnosis,[3] but that doesn't make it any less real or valid. Trauma can stem not only from witnessing death or enduring personal violence, but also from being exposed to other acute or persistent events. This broader understanding has led to the recognition of financial trauma as its own phenomenon, deserving careful attention.

It's my hope that this book deepens your understanding of the many dimensions of financial trauma. From that understanding arises the power to ask whether your relationship with money truly supports your life today or still reflects past survival strategies. Awareness of that distinction is the foundation for true healing.

Reflection Prompt

Have you ever felt emotionally flooded, ashamed, or stuck when dealing with money and wondered if those feelings might come from something deeper than numbers alone?

Why Financial Trauma Matters

A large number of Americans identify as having experienced financial trauma. In a 2023 survey, 68% of adults self-reported enduring it now or in the past.[4]

This aligns with broader research showing economic concerns as a major stressor. In a 2024 survey by the American Psychological Association, 73% of respondents identified the economy (inflation, unemployment) as a "significant source of stress."[5]

This prevalence is troubling because financial trauma profoundly affects quality of life. As we'll see in upcoming chapters, a heightened stress response keeps the body in a chronic state of alert and affects every part of life: mental, physical, relational, spiritual, and more. Over time, trauma can lead to coping mechanisms that ironically deepen financial instability rather than relieve it.

Who This Book Is For

This book is for anyone who's experienced severe financial stress or trauma, even if they don't yet see themselves that way. It's also valuable for people supporting someone through recovery and for professionals curious about the lasting impact of financial adversities. Whether you're searching for personal insight and healing, hoping to better understand a loved one or client, or simply exploring this topic, you'll find useful perspectives here.

When I use "you" throughout this book, I'm speaking to readers who've faced financial stress or trauma. But whether you've lived it yourself or you're here to understand it better, you're in the right place.

Beyond Traditional Financial Advice

This isn't a book about budgets, spreadsheets, or investment strategies. You won't find step-by-step plans for building a retirement fund or cutting expenses. Instead, this book emphasizes a holistic, trauma-informed approach to understanding your relationship with money.

A trauma-informed approach means we won't push quick fixes or shame you for past choices. Instead, we'll look at your money patterns with curiosity and compassion. We'll explore what lies beneath the surface: fear, guilt, survival patterns. From there, we create space for healing, not just behavior change.

The goal isn't just to fix the numbers. It's to ease ingrained nervous system responses so you can move forward with clarity, strength, and self-trust.

Think of this book as your guide to understanding how past events cast a shadow on present financial beliefs, feelings, and responses. More importantly, it will show how awareness can spark lasting change.

Common Causes and Effects of Financial Trauma

Financial trauma can come from many sources. Recognizing these pathways helps normalize our experiences and reminds us there's no single "right way" to develop financial trauma.

Multiple Pathways to Financial Trauma

Financial trauma can take root through several distinct pathways, each capable of creating lasting wounds on its own:

Chronic financial stress arises from ongoing money pressures that never seem to let up. Living paycheck to paycheck, struggling to cover basic needs, or enduring long-term instability can overwhelm the nervous system's ability to cope. The relentlessness itself can be traumatizing, even without one dramatic event. While not all financial stress rises to the level of trauma, research recognizes that cumulative exposure to stressors over time can have traumatic effects.[6]

Acute financial events are sudden shocks that threaten security. Job loss, bankruptcy, foreclosure, investment collapse, business failure, financial fraud, or a major unexpected expense can destabilize life overnight. These moments can be traumatic no matter your prior circumstances.

Financial abuse occurs when money becomes a weapon of control, manipulation, or punishment. Examples include restricting access to funds, sabotaging employment, or forcing dependence to maintain power. This form of abuse creates its own unique trauma pattern.

Systemic and intergenerational factors reflect the wider forces that shape financial lives: discrimination, institutional barriers, inherited beliefs, or generational poverty or instability that feels inescapable. Repeated exposure to these threats instills deep financial wounds that can echo across time.

Vicarious financial trauma develops from witnessing others' financial struggles or hearing repeated stories of hardship. A child who observes constant parental stress, an adult who watches family members lose homes, or anyone regularly exposed to financial crises may develop their own trauma responses.

These pathways aren't ranked in any order. One doesn't have to lead to another, nor is one more valid than the rest. They can appear alone or in combination. Not even people with wealth are immune to financial trauma.

Understanding these pathways allows us to see that no matter how your relationship with money was hurt, the pain is legitimate. The next step is exploring how financial trauma shows up in everyday life.

Effects of Financial Trauma

Financial trauma manifests in many ways, shaping how we think, feel, and behave around money. These responses mirror the recognized symptom patterns seen across different types of trauma.[7]

Cognitive impacts include trouble concentrating on financial information, memory gaps around money matters, or racing thoughts that make clear financial thinking nearly impossible.

Avoidance behaviors might look like postponing financial tasks, ignoring bank statements, delaying important decisions, or disengaging from money management altogether. This protective response can bring temporary relief but often deepens problems over time.

Hypervigilance and anxiety show up as constantly worrying about money, obsessively checking accounts, hoarding resources, or even experiencing physical symptoms (racing heart, sweating, difficulty breathing) when dealing with financial matters.

Emotional overwhelm can make even small money tasks feel crushing. Bills, budgets, or financial conversations may trigger panic, shutdown, detachment from reality, or emotional flooding that feels out of proportion to the situation.

Behavioral responses vary widely and may include:

- Overspending to cope with emotions or to compensate for lack
- Underspending and compulsive saving that sacrifice quality of life for security
- Self-sabotaging when financial progress feels unfamiliar or threatening
- Hiding financial information from others
- Avoiding financial planning or budgeting
- Underearning
- Overworking ("workaholism")

Physical symptoms may include headaches, digestive issues, sleep problems, or chronic muscle tension.

Shame and self-worth issues often ride alongside financial trauma, giving rise to stories of failure, inadequacy, or being "bad with money."

Self-sabotage patterns can emerge when financial success feels somehow unsafe, undeserved, or disconnected from our identity. Without our full awareness, we may undermine our progress just as things begin to improve.

Mental health challenges and financial trauma often form a vicious cycle: Mental health issues can make people more vulnerable to financial trauma, while financial difficulties can trigger or intensify mental health conditions through chronic stress or relationship strain.

Relational effects describe how we connect with others around money. People living with financial trauma may struggle to talk openly about money, argue with partners, isolate due to shame, or wrestle with blurred financial boundaries.

Survivor's guilt often weighs on those who've gained financial stability while family or community members continue to struggle. This guilt can lead to decisions that maintain connection to hardship rather than embrace growth.

The effects of financial trauma aren't just theoretical; they ripple through real lives, including my own. Financial trauma rarely shows up in a single moment; it often layers over time. In my case, each episode was of a different nature, but together they stacked until I realized the problem wasn't just my money management. Something deeper was at work.

That realization pushed me to explore what was really happening beneath the numbers. In this book, I share pieces of my own story alongside the stories of others whose details have been changed or combined to protect their privacy. My hope is that if you recognize yourself here, you'll know you're not alone. This book is meant to help you understand what you're experiencing, ease the emotional distress, and access tools you can start using right away. It also lays the foundation for deeper healing if you choose that path.

Can anyone ever be fully "healed" from trauma, as if they never experienced it? Probably not. But healing can mean something else: shrinking its power, integrating its lessons, and reclaiming your life in meaningful and empowering ways.

You'd never choose to experience trauma. And you shouldn't have had to endure it. But when it does happen, it can sometimes become a catalyst for growth. Post-traumatic growth goes beyond recovery; it's a transformation in values, perspectives, actions, and sense of purpose. It's the kind of shift that can leave you not just surviving but thriving: living with greater wisdom and impact than if you'd never experienced the trauma.

How This Book Is Organized

This book is the first in a comprehensive two-volume series on healing financial trauma. Though part of a set, it stands complete on its own.

It helps you understand what financial trauma is, where it began in your life, and how it continues to affect you today. You'll gain insight into money wounds you may never have named before. The book also shines light on the beliefs, behaviors, and blocks that keep you stuck. And it offers strategies for reducing their impact.

Healing requires this foundational understanding first. Rushing ahead to advanced techniques without understanding the "why" often leads to frustration, failed attempts, and more of the shame that accompanies trauma.

My aim is to give you what you may need right now: a clear framework and practical tools to start easing the weight of financial trauma. If, at some point, you choose to explore more advanced approaches, those resources await in the second volume.

This book is organized into five clusters:

1. Building a Foundation (Chapters 1 to 3)
These chapters unpack how science, psychology, and social context intertwine to shape our money wounds. Together they paint a full picture of how financial trauma develops and takes root.

2. Expanding the Context (Chapters 4 and 5)
This section widens the lens to systemic and cultural forces that shape financial experiences and introduces the ripple effects of key money moments. Recognizing these influences helps reduce self-blame and sets the stage for understanding the patterns that follow.

3. Exploring Consequences (Chapters 6 to 8)
Here you'll explore how financial trauma shows up in daily life, fueling cycles of shame, driving self-sabotage, and sometimes taking the form of complex trauma. You'll begin to see patterns you may not have connected to your money experiences.

4. Uncovering Relationship Dynamics (Chapters 9 to 11)
These chapters show how money wounds intersect with mental health, relationships, and survivor's guilt. They highlight the interpersonal complexities of healing.

5. Bringing It All Together (Chapter 12)
The final chapter consolidates your insights as you move forward with awareness.

This visual roadmap illustrates the journey you'll take through this book:

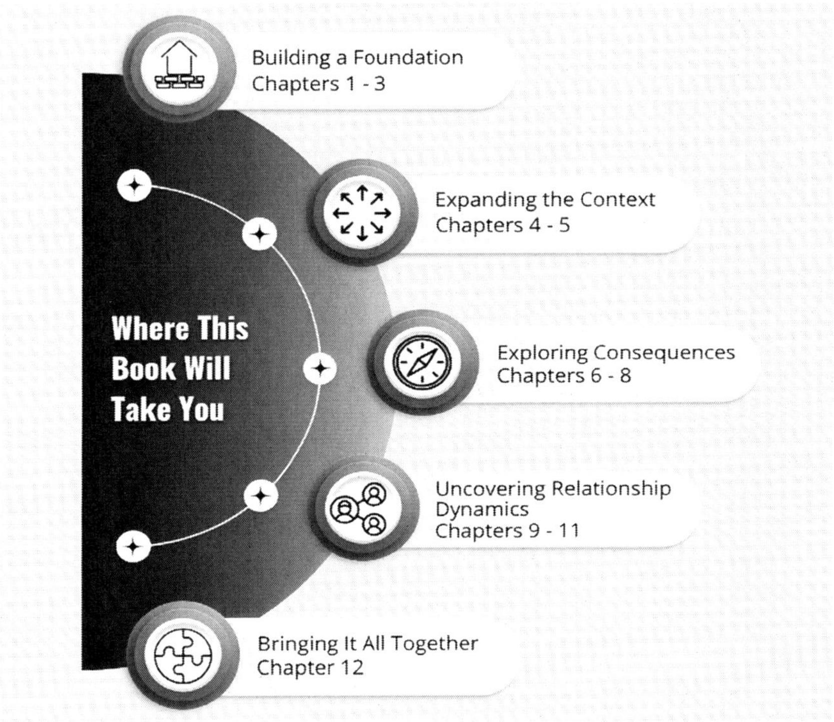

As you move through each section, you'll not only gain insight into financial trauma but also uncover strategies and tools to support your healing. This journey focuses on transformation, not just information. Here's what you can expect to gain along the way.

What You'll Gain from the Book

By engaging with this book, you'll develop deeper self-awareness around your money thoughts, emotions, nervous system responses, and behaviors. You may discover that your struggles have a name, *financial trauma*, and that others share similar experiences.

That realization can be profoundly relieving. Many people carry the belief they're uniquely broken or simply "terrible with money." This book shifts the question from *What's wrong with me?* to *What happened to me?*

That shift matters. It validates that your struggles are real and your responses make sense. You're not a victim of your circumstances or choices. You're an adaptive survivor whose protective strategies are ready to evolve. Feeling understood creates the safety needed for deeper healing work. Without that foundation, it's difficult to engage effectively with trauma recovery.

Along the way, you'll also find practical strategies to ease emotional distress in the moment. These are simple tools you can start using right now, even if you're not considering doing deeper work.

Remember, healing from financial trauma is deeply personal. It happens at its own pace.

How to Use This Book

Each chapter in this book examines a specific aspect of financial trauma and can be accessed as a standalone resource. The full impact of the book unfolds when exploring all chapters sequentially, but you can also navigate to whatever topics resonate with your current needs or interests.

Some material may feel heavy if you've experienced trauma yourself. Your well-being comes first. Please approach this content in whatever way feels safest for you. Read on your own timetable. Take breaks. Skip any stories if they feel like too much, focusing on the broader insights or practical tools instead. The core strategies remain accessible even if you bypass some details.

Key Takeaways

- Financial trauma is real, common, and deeply intertwined with all dimensions of well-being.
- Both chronic financial stress and specific events can lead to long-term money wounds.
- For those affected, recognizing financial trauma is essential for positive change.

Your Invitation to Transformation

Healing financial trauma doesn't involve quick fixes. Deep down, you already know this. It's a matter of uncovering the roots of issues and equipping yourself with tools to shift your relationship with money from the inside out.

But healing doesn't have to be a grueling, downbeat experience. The process can be filled with exciting moments of joy, discovery, breakthrough, and release. You set the pace. I honor your courage in choosing to explore this path.

Reflection Prompt

What would your life look like if money wounds no longer controlled your emotions, your actions, or your sense of self-worth?

Ready to step forward? The journey begins in our next chapter, where we explore the brain-money connection.

2

The Brain Science Behind Financial Behavior

Money sweeps through our lives like ocean waves, sometimes gently sustaining, sometimes overpowering. Our response to its ebb and flow is shaped by our deepest experiences, the ones that may have shaken our sense of identity, safety, or security. How we handle money carries those imprints.

In this chapter, we'll explore the connection between trauma and financial behavior through the lens of neuroscience. Understanding how trauma changes the brain helps us make sense of why we make certain financial decisions and opens the door to healthier money patterns.

What You'll Learn in This Chapter

- How trauma transforms three key brain regions that influence financial decision-making
- Why routine money tasks, like checking bank balances, can trigger trauma responses even when finances are stable
- How trauma reshapes the brain to crave immediate relief over long-term security
- How the nervous system's survival modes—fight, flight, freeze, and fawn—show up in money behavior
- Practical ways to spot trauma-based patterns in your own financial habits
- How you can rewire your brain's pathways for more helpful financial decisions and behavior

The Neuroscience of Financial Decision-Making

The human brain has a threat-response system that serves as a built-in survival mechanism. It primes the body to react to danger. Financial trauma reshapes this system, and unhelpful money patterns often follow.[8] The effects aren't just psychological. Trauma creates measurable changes in the brain that influence how we approach money.

The Brain's Response to Trauma: A Financial Lens

When trauma rewires our brain's threat-response system, it transforms how we perceive and handle decisions about things that matter to us, including money. Imagine your brain as a sophisticated security system. After experiencing trauma, this system becomes hypervigilant, like a security guard who's been through too many break-ins and now views even routine visitors as threats.

Three regions play the biggest role: the amygdala (your emotional alarm), the prefrontal cortex (your planner and decision-maker), and the hippocampus (your memory processor).[9]

Brain Science Simplified

Think of your brain regions as a financial management team:

- **Amygdala: The security guard** (alerts to danger)
- **Prefrontal cortex: The manager** (plans and decides)
- **Hippocampus: The historian** (stores and retrieves relevant memories)

Trauma can push the guard into overdrive, overwhelm the manager, and confuse the historian. The result? A financial team that struggles to work together.

Key Brain Regions Affected by Financial Trauma

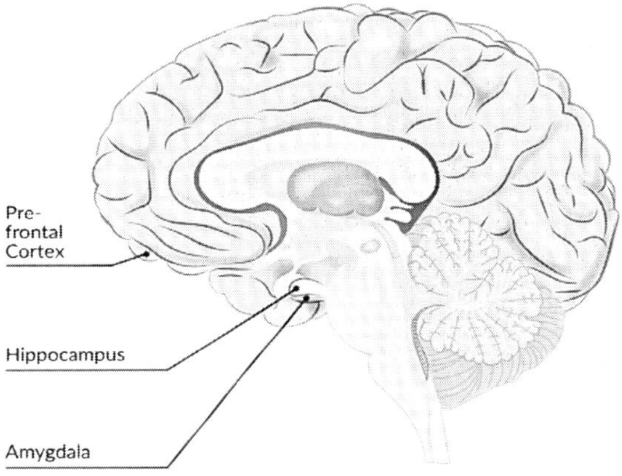

After trauma, the **amygdala** goes into high-alert mode, like an alarm that won't stop ringing. Even basic tasks, like opening bills, can feel like danger. Your heart may race and your palms may sweat, even when you know you're financially stable.

The **prefrontal cortex**, the logical "thinking" part of your brain, also takes a hit. You might make snap money decisions, cave to impulse spending, or struggle to weigh today's choices against tomorrow's needs. It's not a lack of financial literacy or willpower. The decision-making center is overloaded.

The **hippocampus**, your memory center, falters too. Normally it draws on past experiences to weigh current options and guide future choices. After trauma, that process breaks down. You might find yourself forgetting previous financial lessons or feeling unable to apply past experiences to current money decisions. This is why financial choices become harder, especially when comparing similar options, as the ability to ponder and foresee consequences grows cloudy.

The hippocampus also struggles with properly "filing" traumatic financial memories. Instead of being stored as completed past events, these memories can feel raw and current.[10] That's why a credit card statement today can trigger the same dread you felt years ago during a crisis, even if your finances have recovered. Your brain hasn't fully recognized that the old threat is over.

Now that we've met your brain's financial response team, let's take a closer look at what happens when that team stays stuck in crisis mode.

When Your Brain Stays in Financial Survival Mode

Think of survival mode as your brain's emergency protocol: It's useful in a true crisis but creates problems when it becomes your default setting.

We've compared the **amygdala** to an alarm. During a traumatic event, this alarm does its job properly and goes off, signaling extreme danger and helping you escape.

But problems arise because the amygdala and other older parts of the brain are focused on immediate survival, not on long-term logical analysis. They don't have a "reset button" that says, "Okay, that threat is gone now, back to normal." Instead, they can get stuck in a state of high alert because they learned that a particular set of circumstances (sights, sounds, actions, feelings) led to danger.

It's better, from a survival perspective, to have a hundred false alarms than to miss one true threat.[11] That's why the nervous system has a tough time distinguishing between a past danger and present safety. It's a system designed for a primitive world where a missed signal could mean death, and it takes time and intentional effort to help the system re-learn that you're now safe.

After trauma, this state of high alert can linger, shaping your financial life in key ways:

The Brain Becomes Hypersensitive

The brain's alarm system doesn't just learn to fear physical threats. It also learns to associate certain patterns, like financial instability or a lack of control over money, with feelings of danger and helplessness.

Huntley's Story: As a child, Huntley experienced financial trauma after her father suddenly lost his job. She now associates unexpected financial changes with danger. Even a positive event like a recent surprise bonus triggered anxiety, a racing heart, and a tight stomach. An inner voice whispered: *Now something bad will happen.* To cope, she spent the money quickly, not out of recklessness but as an unconscious attempt to gain a sense of control.

The Brain Prioritizes Immediate Relief Over Long-Term Planning

Trauma pushes the brain to choose present safety over future security. Financially, that might look like:

- Keeping too much cash in low-interest accounts instead of investing
- Making impulse purchases to soothe distress
- Avoiding financial planning because it feels overwhelming

Hana's Story: After losing her job in a company-wide layoff, Hana couldn't plan beyond a month ahead. Even after landing a better-paying job, she kept all her money in cash and short-term accounts, avoiding retirement or long-term investments. What might look like caution was really her brain clinging to immediate access in case another crisis struck.

The Brain's Ability to Assess Risk Gets Skewed

Trauma can distort how you evaluate threats and opportunities. You may:

- Overestimate the chances of financial loss
- Undervalue your ability to recover
- Miss opportunities because of excessive caution

Jared's Story: After credit card fraud that took months to resolve, Jared developed intense anxiety about online transactions. He began paying all bills by check and refused digital banking. This "protection strategy" left him vulnerable to late fees and made his financial life harder than it needed to be.

Financial Behavior May Swing Between Extremes

Feeling financially unsafe can lead to polarized behaviors, often swinging between over-control and avoidance:

- Over-control: Monitoring every penny with exhausting precision: a hypervigilant response that seeks safety through control
- Avoidance: Abstaining from financial tasks altogether: a shutdown response that seeks relief through disengagement

When a threat is detected, survival instincts can dictate which response feels safest at any given moment. The brain and body adjust their protective strategies, sometimes opting for control, other times for disengagement, based on what feels survivable in the moment.

Reflection Prompt

Do you notice yourself swinging between over-control and avoidance with money? What might those responses be trying to protect you from?

Recognizing Your Financial Survival Patterns

Understanding the brain science behind trauma responses is valuable, but the real change begins when you spot these patterns in your own financial life. Our brain's ancient survival modes—fight, flight, freeze, and fawn—show up in money decisions more often than we realize.[12]

Your Nervous System's Financial Defense Modes

FIGHT

Financial Threat Confrontation

- Making aggressive, risky investments
- Negotiating combatively
- Confronting others about money
- Monitoring accounts and markets obsessively

FLIGHT

Financial Avoidance

- Neglecting bills and account statements
- Postponing financial decisions
- Using shopping to escape stress
- Changing the subject when money is discussed

FREEZE

Financial Paralysis

- Keeping excessive cash reserves
- Remaining in financially damaging situations
- Feeling paralyzed about money choices
- Planning without taking action

FAWN

Financial People-Pleasing

- Lending money despite strain
- Overspending to preserve ties
- Avoiding financial boundaries with others
- Making money choices to get approval

These responses once served as survival mechanisms but may not serve our current financial well-being.

Fight Response: Taking on Financial Threats

When money feels threatening, some of us instinctively move into "fight" mode. This might mean chasing high-risk investments, getting combative in money conversations, or obsessively tracking account balances or monitoring market movements.

Take Gene, who grew frustrated with fierce competition in real estate investing. His fight response drove him to use aggressive negotiation tactics that damaged business relationships and clouded his judgment about property values. The response gave him a sense of control, but it undermined his financial success.

Flight Response: Financial Avoidance

Others run from money stress. This shows up as ignoring bills, avoiding account balances, postponing big financial decisions, or seeking distraction through spending.

Jesse followed this pattern. When friends or family tried to discuss his mounting debt, he quickly changed the subject or found excuses to leave the room. Avoidance gave him temporary relief but allowed his debt to spiral, making the problem harder to face later.

Freeze Response: Financial Paralysis

Sometimes, overwhelming financial situations trigger a freeze response in the brain's emotional survival system. This can manifest as keeping excessive cash reserves rather than investing, remaining in financially damaging situations out of fear, or experiencing decision paralysis about money choices.

Marissa's story illustrates this pattern. Stuck in an unhappy marriage, she made endless lists of potential actions such as job searches, apartment options, and budget plans. But she was unable to take any steps toward financial independence. Her brain's survival response kept her frozen in place, even as she understood the need for change.

Fawn Response: Financial People-Pleasing

The fawn response gets less attention than the others, but it's common in money behavior. It can mean lending money you can't spare, overspending on gifts to keep relationships smooth, or avoiding setting boundaries with friends and loved ones.

Della's experience illustrates this. When a friend asked her for money to start a new business, Della feared that requesting a formal contract might jeopardize the relationship. She waived a written agreement, choosing a sense of emotional safety over financial clarity. Her fawn response left her financially exposed.

Trust and Financial Relationships

Two brain regions affected by trauma, the amygdala and the prefrontal cortex, also play a role in social trust. Trauma changes not only how you read financial threats but also how you interpret people's cues in money conversations.

That's why a financial chat with family can feel more intense than expected, or why sitting down with an advisor sparks anxiety. Your brain's "social radar" is on high alert, making it harder to build the trusting, collaborative relationships that support financial well-being.

Cultivating Self-Compassion About Financial Responses

Recognizing these patterns isn't about judging yourself. These responses developed to protect you from your original trauma. They helped you survive. The challenge now is to see when they're no longer serving your financial well-being. With awareness and self-kindness, you can start shifting toward more balanced ways of handling money.

The Path Forward: Neuroplasticity and Financial Healing

Just as rivers carve new paths, your brain can forge new neural connections through a process known as *neuroplasticity,* or the brain's ability to adapt and change. Trauma may have created certain financial response patterns, but you're capable of updating them. The same adaptability that helped you survive trauma can now help you heal.

Breaking Free: The First Step

Understanding these patterns is like learning to read a river's current. Navigators don't fight the water; they study its flow. When you recognize how trauma has shaped your financial responses, you can ask whether your habits serve your present needs or simply echo old survival strategies.

Like a river redirected, your financial patterns can shift once you understand their source. This awareness isn't about damming the flow of your experiences. It's about steering them with more intention and care.

The Healing Brain and Financial Recovery

The brain's ability to heal is remarkable. With consistent practice, new pathways form that support healthier financial responses. Healing doesn't happen overnight, but it builds over time.

Research on neuroplasticity shows the brain reorganizes itself throughout life, creating new connections as we learn. Psychologist Rick Hanson calls this "taking in the good": deliberately focusing on positive experiences to strengthen resilience.[13]

Applied to money, this means each positive action, no matter how small, helps reshape your brain. Every time you engage with finances without overwhelming stress, you're laying down healthier neural pathways.

Reflection Questions: Recognizing Your Financial Response Patterns

Take a moment to pause and consider:

Do you see yourself in any of the trauma responses: fight, flight, freeze, or fawn? Which patterns would you most like to shift?

When you make financial choices that don't align with your long-term goals, what emotions or body sensations arise? These signals often point to trauma responses at work.

Observing your patterns without judgment is a powerful beginning. In the chapters ahead, we'll explore tools for working with these responses in practical, everyday ways.

Key Takeaways

- The brain-money connection is real: Trauma reshapes brain function in ways that make money tasks feel more threatening than they are.
- Your heightened stress responses aren't a personal flaw but rather your brain's attempt to keep you safe; understanding this can reduce self-judgment.

- Survival mode can protect you in the short term but often undermines long-term financial health.
- The brain's ability to adapt and form new connections offers hope for a more positive relationship with money.

As we move into Chapter 3, we'll explore how thought patterns begin in childhood. Early experiences and messages about money shape the foundation for adult financial beliefs. To understand your current patterns, we'll first trace them back to where they began.

3

Early Lessons: How Childhood Shapes Adult Money Patterns

Like a river carving its path, our earliest experiences with money shape lasting patterns. These encounters can create deep channels that guide our financial decisions for decades. Just as water follows the path of least resistance, we often unconsciously follow these early-formed financial patterns until we finally become aware of them and can redirect their course.

In this chapter, we'll explore how childhood experiences shape money beliefs and behaviors. When you see how deeply these patterns run, it becomes clear why a new budget or investment plan isn't enough. Lasting change requires understanding where your money patterns came from and then intentionally reshaping these ingrained channels.

What You'll Learn in This Chapter

Your early experiences with money influence your financial life in ways that often remain hidden until you shine a light on them. In this chapter, you'll discover:

- How childhood experiences create lasting beliefs about money and why family attitudes toward finances echo through generations
- The ways early trauma influences adult money decisions and how to begin recognizing your own financial patterns
- Practical tools for rewriting unhelpful money scripts and building a healthier connection with money
- How childhood patterns connect with broader cultural and societal influences

The Invisible Inheritance: How Childhood Shapes Money Beliefs

Think of your early money experiences as an invisible inheritance, a set of unwritten rules and beliefs passed down by parents and caregivers, sometimes across multiple generations. Psychologists call these your money scripts, deeply rooted imprints that act like an emotional blueprint for your financial decisions. Sometimes, these scripts lead to healthy habits like disciplined saving or careful investing, while other times they can create lasting burdens.

Take Nita. When she was eight, her parents lost their home during a financial crisis. Now, even as a successful adult with a steady income, she keeps six savings accounts and panics if any of them dip below a certain threshold. Her behavior isn't really about the numbers. It's about the fear she's carried since childhood. Saving has become a bandage for old wounds.

Her story illustrates how childhood experiences lay down brain pathways that connect money to survival, safety, and self-worth. Even when adult circumstances look nothing like those of childhood, the early imprints often continue to guide financial choices. By understanding the roots of her habits, Nita can begin to ease her sense of scarcity and prevent those hidden beliefs from shaping her children's money patterns.

How Money Scripts Form in the Developing Brain

Money scripts are hardwired into our brains from our earliest years, often during a crucial period of development. During early and middle childhood, a child's brain is rapidly learning how to interpret the world, but it does so largely through an **emotional lens** rather than a logical one. The connections between the amygdala, the brain's emotional alarm system, and the prefrontal cortex, the center for rational thought, are still maturing during this period and won't reach adult-like patterns until adolescence.[14]

This means many early money lessons become emotional memories rather than rational ones. A six-year-old who watches parents fight about money might only grasp fragments of the argument, but the emotional imprint, *Money equals conflict*, sticks. Years later, even casual conversations about finances could trigger undue stress if that child experienced financial trauma over their parents' conflict.

Children tend to think in concrete, absolute ways and often make black-and-white interpretations of complex events.[15] For instance, a family tightening the budget after a job change might lead a child to conclude: *Money is always scarce* or *We'll never afford what we want.* These simplified interpretations can harden into enduring money scripts, long after circumstances improve.

These early impressions become the foundation of your adult relationship with money, quietly shaping decisions and emotions, often without your awareness.

Childhood experiences create both cognitive beliefs (money scripts) and embodied nervous system responses. These aren't separate phenomena. They're two sides of the same coin. The emotional intensity of early financial experiences gets stored in both our thinking patterns and our nervous systems. A trauma-informed approach recognizes that lasting change requires addressing both the beliefs we hold about money and the nervous system responses that get triggered around financial situations.

The Integration of Belief and Body

Financial trauma runs deeper than money beliefs. It lives in the nervous system, where survival patterns form around financial stress. When children grow up in conditions that threaten their sense of safety about money, their brains develop both a story about what money means and a survival response to financial situations. True financial recovery requires addressing both dimensions.

Family Money Messages: The Hidden Curriculum

Your family served as your first financial education system, teaching you not just how to handle money, but also what money means. These lessons came through both direct instruction and subtle cues:

Spoken Messages

Explicit statements you might have heard:

- "Money is the root of all evil."
- "Stop dreaming; no one in *our* family tree ever gets rich."

- "Money will solve all our problems."
- "Never talk about money."
- "You can't take it with you."
- "Debt is just a tool. Everyone uses it."
- "We've got to downplay our wealth or people will treat us differently."
- "Rich people are greedy."
- "You have to work hard for every penny."

Unspoken Messages

The lessons you absorbed by observing:

- Parents hiding purchases from each other
- Tension during bill-paying time
- Celebrations or conflicts around paydays or bonuses
- The gap between what parents said about money and how they behaved
- Who made financial decisions in the household
- Which expenses were prioritized, and which were dismissed as "wasteful"

Sometimes, too, money lessons come through painful events. When a child lacks the tools to process an emotional wound, their mind often creates a story to explain what happened and to avoid future pain. For instance, a child whose parent loses their job might internalize the belief that *financial security is an illusion* after witnessing their family's sudden shift from stability to instability. That belief can later fuel chronic anxiety, even when adult finances are objectively stable.

Together, these spoken and unspoken lessons form deep associations that influence adult behavior. If money talks at home always ended in conflict, you might now avoid financial conversations with your partner, even when openness would strengthen your relationship.

This hidden curriculum explains why conventional advice like "track your spending" often fails. It addresses surface behavior but ignores what lies beneath. These inherited money scripts act like invisible currents, pulling you toward familiar shores, even when you're determined to set a new course.

To truly understand how childhood experiences shape adult money behaviors, we need to look beyond beliefs and examine how early trauma embeds itself in the nervous system. The sections ahead on generational and individual money patterns reveal how childhood experiences create lasting behavioral responses. These aren't just ways of thinking about money. They're embodied survival strategies, carried forward from times when the world felt financially unsafe.

Money Scripts Across Generations: The Family Financial Legacy

Money scripts often travel across generations, carrying the emotional imprint of experiences you never lived through. For example:

First Generation: They lose everything during an economic depression, enduring true financial devastation.

Second Generation: Growing up hearing stories about "the hard times," this generation becomes intensely frugal and hypervigilant: working multiple jobs, saving obsessively, and avoiding risk at all costs.

Third Generation: With little knowledge of the original crisis but raised by parents wired for scarcity, this generation inherits money anxiety without context. They may either continue the family's cautious habits or swing in the opposite direction, rebelling against what feels like irrational fears.

Patterns like these explain why families often cling to financial behaviors long after their purpose has disappeared. You may have grown up in relative stability yet still absorbed scripts like "always keep cash hidden" or "never trust banks" from relatives whose worldview was shaped by economic collapse, even if you didn't know their story.

Generational patterns also reflect cultural and socioeconomic realities. Immigrant families, for example, often carry scripts influenced by both their countries of origin and their struggle to navigate new systems. Likewise, families from historically marginalized communities may develop unique financial worldviews as survival responses to systemic barriers that persist across generations.

Building on Financial Psychology: From Money Scripts to Trauma Patterns

Financial psychologist Dr. Brad Klontz introduced the concept of money scripts, unconscious beliefs about money formed in childhood that guide adult behaviors.[16] He identified four core types:

- **Money Avoidance**: Believing money is bad or corrupting
- **Money Worship**: Believing money solves all problems
- **Money Status**: Equating net worth with self-worth
- **Money Vigilance**: Feeling constant anxiety or suspicion around money

This book builds on Dr. Klontz's foundation by exploring how money scripts exist not only as thoughts but as embodied patterns shaped by trauma. When we understand how trauma responses shape our financial lives, we can finally make sense of behaviors that have puzzled us for years.

Through this trauma lens, money patterns can be seen as survival strategies. Some people overwork to feel safe (*fight*). Others avoid budgeting or bills because they feel overwhelmed (*flight*). Still others shut down when facing financial tasks (*freeze*). And some people defer to others in financial decisions, hoping to keep the peace (*fawn*).

A trauma lens is a complementary perspective to Klontz's foundational work and directly connects the dots between belief, body, and behavior. It explains why financial decisions can feel like life-or-death situations, even when the stakes look small on paper. This approach can offer hope and a fresh direction if conventional financial counseling or education has been ineffective for you.

In the next section, we'll explore four common trauma-informed money patterns, each rooted in emotional wounds from the past, each still shaping adult financial lives.

Four Common Patterns: How Early Experiences Shape Adult Behavior

In working with financial trauma, I've observed four common scripts that appear to trace back to childhood financial experiences: the Over-Controller, the Avoider, the Rescuer, and the Risk-Taker. These patterns show how trauma responses play out in financial life, carrying forward family dynamics and survival strategies long after childhood has ended.

The Over-Controller

Core Belief: "Financial security requires constant vigilance."

Childhood Origins: Over-Controllers often come from environments marked by:

- Financial insecurity or sudden downturns
- Unpredictable or inconsistent money flow
- A heavy emphasis on being "responsible" with finances

Appearance in Adult Life:

- Creating and obsessively following detailed budgets
- Checking balances multiple times a day
- Feeling anxious about spending on non-essentials
- Struggling to enjoy wealth, even when secure
- Being overly concerned with saving for worst-case scenarios
- Resisting spontaneity with money

Pattern in Action: Marcus grew up watching his single mother juggle debt after his father left. Now, as a well-paid architect with significant savings, he still tracks every expense in color-coded spreadsheets and feels physically uneasy (muscle tension, shallow breathing) making unplanned purchases. He has turned down invitations to vacations with friends, labeling the trips as "irresponsible," despite being able to easily afford them.

The Trauma Connection *(Nervous System Response—Hypervigilance)*: The nervous system treats routine financial situations as potential emergencies. Financial behaviors go far beyond prudent habits and become unconscious attempts to create safety in a world the nervous system still perceives as financially threatening.

The Protective Paradox: Extreme diligence creates stability, but often at the expense of joy, spontaneity, and connection. Money is managed perfectly but rarely enjoyed.

The Avoider

Core Belief: "Money is overwhelming, confusing, or unsafe."

Childhood Origins: Avoiders may grow up in households where:

- Money talk led to conflict or felt threatening.
- Financial matters were handled secretly or treated as taboo.
- Messages about wealth were inconsistent.
- Financial concepts weren't explained.
- Money carried shame, guilt, or fear.

Appearance in Adult Life:

- Procrastinating on bills or taxes
- Ignoring financial statements
- Having little awareness of overall finances
- Making decisions impulsively, not strategically
- Delegating financial matters to others
- Showing a puzzling gap between financial knowledge and other life competencies

Pattern in Action: Despite excelling at complex projects in her career, Leila panics when faced with financial tasks. She has three old retirement accounts she's never consolidated and relies on her partner to manage household finances. Even simple money conversations leave her emotional or eager to change the subject.

The Trauma Connection *(Nervous System Response—Freeze/Shutdown)*: For Avoiders, the nervous system becomes overwhelmed and shuts down as a protective mechanism. This manifests as brain fog during financial conversations, physical heaviness or fatigue when bills arrive, procrastination that feels almost paralytic, or a sense of disconnection from the body during money-related activities.

The Protective Paradox: Avoidance shields you from immediate distress but leaves you exposed in the long run. The relief is temporary, while the financial consequences accumulate.

The Rescuer

Core Belief: "My worth is tied to how much I financially help others."

Childhood Origins: Rescuers often grow up where:

- They assumed adult responsibility early.
- They were praised for being "helpful" or "responsible."
- Money was tied to care, love, or approval.
- Family or community struggled financially.
- Caretakers modeled self-sacrifice for others.

Appearance in Adult Life:

- Lending money at personal cost
- Struggling to say no to requests

- Prioritizing others' needs above personal stability
- Feeling responsible for solving others' money problems
- Experiencing guilt when setting financial boundaries
- Using money to maintain closeness or ensure usefulness

Pattern in Action: As the oldest of four in a low-income family, Damon contributed his lawn-mowing money to the household from age 12. Now an adult with a high salary, he co-signs relatives' loans, pays his brother's rent, and regularly hands out money to friends. His own retirement savings are minimal because others' needs always come first.

The Trauma Connection *(Nervous System Response—Hyperarousal/Fawn)***:** The nervous system becomes activated by others' financial distress, creating an urgent need to "fix" the situation to restore internal calm. This shows up as physical agitation when hearing about others' money problems and a compulsive drive to take action. If you've achieved financial stability while family or community members continue to struggle, you may feel driven by Survivor's Guilt (see Chapter 11) to try to rescue them. This pattern reflects how financial trauma can become entangled with our sense of identity and worth.

The Protective Paradox: Rescuing can create meaningful support for loved ones, but it can erode financial security and healthy boundaries. The urge to protect others may eventually strip you of the ability to help anyone, including yourself.

The Risk-Taker

Core Belief: "Big rewards require big risks."

Childhood Origins: Risk-Takers often grow up in environments where:

- Access to money was restricted or controlled.
- They saw dramatic wins from gambling, investments, business, or other high-stakes ventures.
- Money represented freedom or escape.
- Financial role modeling was inconsistent.

Appearance in Adult Life:

- Making impulsive financial moves
- Favoring high-risk investments or ventures
- Using money as a tool for identity or status
- Struggling to build stable savings
- Experiencing boom-and-bust cycles
- Showing overconfidence despite losses

Pattern in Action: Alex's father always chased a "big break," while his mother pinched every penny. He remembers the constant tension in the house, the emotional highs of a win, and the crushing and enduring lows of a loss. As an adult, Alex cycles between entrepreneurial ventures, often investing his entire savings into new business ideas without adequate planning. He's had both spectacular successes and devastating failures. Even after bankruptcy, he remains convinced his next idea will change everything. He drives an expensive car but sometimes can't cover rent.

The Trauma Connection *(Nervous System Response—Alternating between Hyperarousal and Crash)***:** Although sharing some elements with Klontz's Money Worship and Money Status scripts, the Risk-Taker pattern is also an attempt to regulate the nervous system. This pattern distracts and numbs. The intense focus on the game, the stock market, or the thrill of the purchase pulls attention away from internal distress. Risky financial behavior can also be used to "discharge" trauma-based hyperarousal. It's not just money Risk-Takers are after. They're chasing relief as well.

The Protective Paradox: Boldness can create opportunity, but volatility often follows. Risk-taking delivers distraction and excitement but rarely stability.

When Patterns Overlap: The Complex Reality of Money Scripts

Most people don't fit perfectly into just one pattern. Your financial behavior is complex and often reveals a combination of scripts, sometimes even holding contradictory beliefs simultaneously. You may track every dollar (Over-Controller) yet funnel that money to relatives without question (Rescuer). These contradictions can create inner conflict and stall financial progress.

The complexity of these intertwined patterns shows the nuanced ways trauma and early experiences shape your relationship with money, and acknowledging this is a key step toward integration and healing.

The truth is that financial behavior is rarely simple. It's a layered mix of beliefs, emotions, systemic and cultural influences, nervous system responses, and survival strategies. Looking inward leads to greater self-awareness and money peace.

Reflection Questions: Noticing Your Own Patterns

Think about the financial behavior that causes you the most stress or confusion right now. Which of the four trauma-aware money patterns

(Over-Controller, Avoider, Rescuer, or Risk-Taker), or which combination, might be fueling it?

Instead of judging your actions as "good" or "bad," ask what your money pattern is trying to protect you from. What would it mean to honor the protection it once provided while also acknowledging your current need for something different?

Breaking the Pattern: Recognition as the First Step

When left unexamined, money scripts act like default settings. They steer your decisions, even when those choices no longer serve you. This isn't your fault.

Think of your brain as a landscape full of trails. Old pathways from childhood are clear and well worn. You may automatically follow them, even if they can't take you to your preferred destination. But you're not stuck with them.

Understanding this is the beginning of change.

Start by taking note of your patterns with curiosity, not judgment. Do you slip into familiar activities, even when you realize on some level they're unhelpful? These observations reveal more than frustrating repetitions. They're clues to your financial inheritance. It also helps to bring attention to your emotional and physical responses to money.

As awareness grows, you can begin to reimagine the meaning underneath those patterns and to reshape your money story. The ability of the brain to create new pathways ensures that with intention and repetition, you can replace your outdated scripts with more supportive ones.

Practical Tools: Identifying and Transforming Your Money Scripts

Self-Reflection: Uncovering Your Financial Patterns

As you consider the questions below, notice what surprises you or stirs emotional or physical changes. Those moments often hold the deepest insights. Writing your responses in a journal can help you track them over time and reveal patterns you might otherwise miss.

1. **Family Money Messages:** What spoken or unspoken money lessons did you absorb growing up?
2. **Emotional Triggers:** Which financial situations spark the strongest feelings, like anxiety, avoidance, excitement, or shame? How might these situations connect to your early experiences?
3. **Body Awareness:** What physical sensations do you notice during financial activities? For example, do you experience fidgeting, a pounding heart, sweating, or fatigue? When do these sensations feel strongest, and how might your body be trying to protect you: signaling danger, preparing you to act, or urging you to pause?
4. **Pattern Recognition:** Which of the four patterns (Over-Controller, Avoider, Rescuer, Risk-Taker) feels most familiar? Which causes you the most stress or confusion today? Do you notice elements of more than one?
5. **Current Impact:** How might your early money experiences still be shaping your financial decisions? Where do you suspect your money scripts are limiting you?

Rewriting Your Money Story: A Step-by-Step Process

Once you're aware of your unhelpful inherited patterns, you can use the following steps to replace them with something that serves you better. View these ideas as simply a suggestion, not a prescription.

1. **Target an Unwanted Script:** Choose a money statement you suspect is limiting you. Example: *I don't deserve financial success.*
2. **Trace Its Origins:** Ask when and how it began. Was it taught, observed, or born from hardship? If you don't know now, that's okay. Awareness will come with time.
3. **Assess Its Validity:** Does this script fit your current reality? Does it reflect your values and serve your goals? Or is it a relic of past circumstances?
4. **Notice Your Body's Response:** Pay attention to how your body reacts to both the old pattern and potential new ones. Does the old script create tension or heaviness? Does a new possibility bring a sense of lightness or expansion? Let your nervous system guide you toward scripts that feel attuned to your whole self.
5. **Create a New Script:** Replace your old pattern with one that supports you today. Example: *I'm learning to accept that I'm worthy of financial well-being and capable of handling it.* Adjust the wording until it feels authentic and achievable.
6. **Practice Daily Reinforcement:** Find ways to remind yourself of this new script through:
    - Affirmations or visual cues (such as Post-it notes or a vision board) that are realistic and evoke emotions you want to associate with this new pattern
    - Small, deliberate actions aligned with the new script

Moving Toward Integration and Growth

Recognizing your money scripts doesn't mean blaming yourself, your parents, or society. The idea is to shift from automatic reaction to conscious choice. The goal isn't to erase your financial past but to evolve into a version of yourself with a healthier, more intentional relationship with money.

This awareness can also change how you relate to others. When you notice the same patterns in family members, you may find new understanding for their behaviors that once left you confused or frustrated. This can soften judgment and open doors to meaningful conversations.

When you look closely, many so-called "bad" financial habits reveal themselves not as character flaws but as survival strategies. Traditional financial education rarely accounts for this truth. But when we see the trauma beneath the behavior, we stop labeling it as weakness or irresponsibility. We recognize it for what it is: a nervous system doing its best to protect us.

In the coming chapters, we'll explore specific strategies for easing trauma responses and developing new financial behaviors that align with your authentic values and goals rather than outdated scripts. We'll also see how these positive changes can create ripple effects across other areas of life, from relationships to career choices to overall well-being.

Remember that rewiring your money patterns takes time. The neural pathways formed over decades won't shift overnight, but change is possible. Be patient with yourself as you continue this process of financial self-discovery and transformation.

Key Takeaways

- Childhood money experiences shape adult financial behavior, even long after circumstances change.
- Spoken and unspoken money lessons can shape behavior across entire lifetimes and even across generations.
- Four common patterns dominate: Over-Controller, Avoider, Rescuer, and Risk-Taker, each one serving protective purposes while also carrying costs.
- Naming your patterns is the first step toward shifting them.
- The same ability of the brain to create protective money patterns can be harnessed to build new, preferred patterns.
- The goal isn't to erase your financial past but to understand it, learn from it, and consciously choose which aspects to carry forward.

The childhood patterns we've explored don't remain frozen in time. They travel with us into adulthood, where they collide with new challenges, responsibilities, and pivotal moments.

In the next chapter, we'll look at how major financial events in adulthood can reopen old money wounds and ripple through every dimension of our well-being.

4

The Ripple Effect: How One Money Moment Can Change Everything

Most adults (68% according to a recent survey) have experienced financial trauma.[17] Significant money events have reshaped how we think, feel, and act around money. These moments become part of our frame of reference, often influencing every dimension of our lives without our conscious awareness.

Money events can lift us up or unsettle us; in this chapter, we'll focus on the ones that test our resilience and shape how we navigate life's uncertainties. Like a stone dropped in a pond, their effects ripple far from the source, touching every part of our lives in ways we may not even notice.

A bankruptcy, for example, might not only drain bank accounts but also trigger chronic stress, foster a scarcity outlook that seeps into relationships, or drive someone to seek stability through a career at the expense of personal fulfillment.

As we explore these events, remember that we're not focusing on the stones themselves. We're tracing the ripples. By noticing these patterns, we can honor the strategies that once kept us safe and gently guide ourselves toward more conscious, empowered choices.

What You'll Learn in This Chapter

- How key financial events in adulthood can affect you and spill into other parts of life
- The ripple effects of financial trauma on eight dimensions of well-being
- How these areas interconnect, creating both challenges and opportunities for healing
- Practical ways to assess your holistic wealth and take aligned action
- Strategies for moving from financial trauma toward balance and empowerment

The Impact of Adult Financial Trauma

Childhood experiences (explored in Chapter 3) lay the foundation for our money beliefs and nervous system responses. But major financial events in adulthood also shape our relationship with money. These adult experiences interact with existing money scripts in complex ways, sometimes reinforcing them, sometimes creating jarring contradictions that force adaptation.

Adult financial trauma often hits where it hurts most: our sense of who we are, who we're responsible for, and what we expected life to give us in return for playing by the rules.

Identity Challenge: Financial stability often intertwines with identity. When identity is threatened, the result can be a crisis of self. A business owner whose company fails might question not only their financial decisions but also their core competence and purpose.

Responsibility Strain: Adults often bear financial responsibility for others, such as children, partners, aging parents, and employees, magnifying the emotional impact of financial setbacks and perceived failure in the role of provider or leader.

Expectation Violation: Many of us carry the belief that if we get a skill or education, work hard, and save diligently, we'll achieve security. When reality breaks that promise through job loss, a market crash, or a health crisis, the dissonance can shake our sense of fairness and predictability in the world.

To navigate these disruptions, we often adapt our money scripts and habits in ways that offer immediate emotional protection but limit long-term recovery. Someone who experiences identity theft, for instance, might adopt extreme security measures that make even routine transactions anxiety-producing and time-consuming.

The good news: As adults, we have more capacity for reflection and integration than we did as children. We can notice these adaptive responses, release them with appreciation for their protection, and choose more balanced perspectives that strengthen our well-being.

The impacts of financial setbacks don't happen in isolation. They weave together in complex patterns that reflect the unique challenges of adult financial trauma. So we'll use a holistic lens to explore how adverse events in adulthood shape our money scripts.

The Effects of Financially Traumatic Events on Holistic Well-Being

A holistic approach views financial health as multidimensional, extending far beyond the numbers in an account. A financial wound creates an imbalance in this system. And in a system, no wound stays contained. Stress in one area inevitably spills into the others.

To help you track these ripple effects in your own life, we'll be using a framework that examines eight dimensions of wellness: ***Emotional, Physical, Vocational, Social, Spiritual, Intellectual, Environmental***, and ***Financial***. At the end of the chapter, you'll have the opportunity to create your own Personal Wealth Dashboard, a visual tool that will help you see where you're thriving and where you might want to focus attention.

As you read the stories in this chapter, you might find it helpful to think about how financial trauma has touched each area of wellness in your own life.

These stories don't capture every possible outcome, but they highlight patterns many people recognize when they've lived through pivotal financial experiences.

Emotional Well-Being

As we saw in Chapter 2, financial trauma can alter brain function, making it harder to understand and regulate our emotions. The result? Heightened emotions like anxiety, anger, fear, shame, guilt, or frustration can toss even simple financial routines off course.

Jen's Story

After twelve years at the same nonprofit, Jen was laid off when the organization lost funding. Shock gave way to depression, anger, grief, and agitation. She spiraled into self-doubt and stopped looking for work.

Later, Jen bumped into a former co-worker who'd also been let go and who mentioned a small group of women meeting monthly to swap leads and vent about the job hunt.

Hearing others at the meeting describe the same emotions Jen felt didn't erase her concerns, but it softened them. By the third meeting, she left with a notebook full of ideas, a spark of motivation, and a sense of peace she hadn't felt in a long time.

Healing Tip

Journaling, attending peer support groups, or working with a trauma-informed professional can help you process emotions.

Connection Question

Looking back, what activities or choices have helped you ease strong emotions?

Physical Well-Being

Financial stress exacts a physical price. Chronic stress can increase the risk of cardiovascular disease, accidents, and poor mental and physical health.[18] About 34% of people report that financial stress negatively affects their sleep. Among them, nearly a quarter experience severe disturbances: nightmares, night terrors, broken sleep, insomnia, or waking up fatigued.[19]

These physical effects create a feedback loop. For example, poor sleep due to money problems impairs cognitive function and emotional regulation, making problem-solving harder and sometimes worsening the original financial situation.

Carlos' Story

When Carlos' rent jumped by 15%, his budget cracked. Groceries, gas, even sleep became harder to manage. He started waking up groggy with headaches and dreading work, worried he'd slip up due to fatigue and lose the job he relied on.

At an office visit, his doctor suggested a few small tools, like a 5-5-5 breathing routine (inhale for 5 seconds, hold for 5 seconds, exhale for 5 seconds) to help soothe his nervous system at night.

Carlos also reached out to a local community garden program. The extra produce helped stretch his budget and nourish his body, and tending the plants brought mild exercise along with unexpected emotional relief.

The physical self-care helped Carlos sleep better and think more clearly. He explored options for dealing with the rent increase and found a roommate. His sleep is consistently better, and he's slowly building an emergency fund.

Healing Tip

Regular self-care and stress-reduction practices can yield tangible results. They help maintain your health and clarity while you work through practical financial solutions.

Connection Question

Where do you notice stress showing up in your body: sleep, energy, digestion, tension? How could easing it help you tackle financial problems more effectively?

Vocational Well-Being

Financial wounds can influence work choices, pushing some people toward low-stress roles, and others toward jobs that offer control or security.[20]

When trauma dictates career choice, misalignment with one's true calling can result in burnout, dissatisfaction, or stalled progress.

Malik's Story

At 19, Malik watched his best friend's family lose their home to foreclosure. The stress tore the family apart, and Malik was deeply affected. Determined to avoid that kind of chaos, Malik switched his college major from education to engineering, hoping for more financial stability.

Now in his 30s, he's successful on paper but restless. His job pays very well, but he yearns for work that allows him to impact others' lives directly. Still, the thought of changing careers fills him with panic. What if he ends up like his friend's parents?

By talking with trusted friends, Malik has been able to name the trauma that's been driving him. For now, he's not changing careers. But he's exploring small ways to reconnect with his dream of teaching: tutoring on weekends, mentoring interns. For the first time in years, he's imagining other possibilities.

Healing Tip

Reflect on whether financial trauma has influenced your career choices and whether they align with your values and desired impact. If necessary, consider gradual shifts toward more fulfilling work while maintaining financial stability.

Connection Question

How might your past financial experiences be shaping your career choices today?

Social Well-Being

Strong social connections support mental health, reduce anxiety and depression, and contribute to a healthier immune system and potentially longer life.[21] But trauma can strain these connections in many ways, whether through financial secrecy, financial abuse, or the self-isolation that comes from money shame.

Stella's Story

After discovering her spouse had secretly racked up massive credit card debt, Stella felt blindsided. Even after the divorce, she carried mistrust and shame into every area of her life, including the social sphere. She declined dinner invitations, worried friends would split checks unfairly or judge her bankruptcy. Even casual conversations about shopping or vacation plans felt loaded with judgment she couldn't shake.

Months later, loneliness began to feel worse than fear. She started volunteering at a local animal shelter. Connecting with people while helping dogs felt safe. She hasn't recovered from her financial betrayal yet, but she's learning that trust can grow in unexpected places.

Healing Tip

Recovery often begins with gentle connection. Reaching out through shared purpose, like volunteering or community activities, can help rebuild trust and remind you that you are worthy of belonging.

Connection Question

Where might you find low-stakes social connections that feel safe while you rebuild trust?

Spiritual or Existential Well-Being

Trauma, including financial trauma, can challenge your faith in life's fundamental goodness and your ability to trust in future provision.

Mick's Story

At 38, Mick lost the dream home he was building and his sense of direction when an industry shake-up toppled the company he'd spent a decade creating. Before the collapse, his life had felt balanced: Sunday volunteer work, regular meditation, and a sense that his business success was meant to serve something larger than himself.

He started over in corporate work to rebuild his finances. But the volunteer work stopped; it felt naive now, like something only people with safety nets could afford. Meditation felt pointless when his mind just circled back to worst-case scenarios. Even after tucking away an emergency fund large enough to survive almost anything, he obsessed over spreadsheets and skipped vacations. The spiritual practices that once grounded him now seemed like luxuries he'd been foolish to indulge.

At an old friend's urging, he did manage to attend a weekend retreat, where he heard a question that stayed with him: *Where does security stop being about control and start being about trust?* He didn't have an answer, but he wanted to figure it out.

Gradually, Mick has made some changes: donations aligned with his beliefs, a return to meditation. He's beginning to believe wealth might mean more than just financial stability.

Healing Tip

Consider connecting with nature, cultivating gratitude, or finding a community focused on generosity or purpose.

Connection Question

Which money beliefs give you meaning? Which ones are you ready to release?

Intellectual Well-Being

As explored in Chapter 2, financial trauma can hijack rational thought, clouding our ability to learn, focus, make decisions, or engage with new money management strategies.

Ruby's Story

After falling for a fraudulent investment, Ruby lost most of her retirement savings. The betrayal stunned her. She stepped back from learning about money because the subject stirred up painful emotions that hijacked her focus.

As the months passed, she continued to avoid financial topics until one day, while inching through traffic, she caught part of an interview with a consumer advocate. He explained how widespread fraud is and how shame silences victims. His words resonated with her, and the following morning she tried something new: reengaging with financial topics in manageable chunks and soothing herself when her emotions flared. She kept it up and even started adding to her retirement account again.

Much later, a suspicious email landed in her inbox and sent a jolt through her system. After she steadied herself, she realized she had spotted the fraud right away. The trigger still stung, but she felt proud of how far she'd come.

Healing Tip

Start with whatever mode of learning that feels right for you. Reading brief articles or listening to podcasts during daily routines is often a comfortable way to ease into a topic.

Connection Question

What financial topics naturally interest you, and how could you explore them further?

Environmental Well-Being

Trauma is a factor in how we relate to our physical spaces and possessions. A history of trauma may lead to clutter or overaccumulation.[22]

Sharon's Story

After years of instability, Sharon struggled to throw anything away. Her apartment overflowed with "just-in-case" items that gave her a sense of control but also left her feeling anxious, embarrassed, and stuck.

One evening, a small kitchen fire began when loose papers near her stove fell onto a burner. A firefighter mentioned downsizing, and though Sharon bristled, the incident shook her. Since then, she's donated a box of clothes and moved flammable stacks. She's thinking. And that, for now, counts as movement.

Healing Tip

Strive to maintain a living space that reflects your values and supports your well-being.

Connection Question

What's one thing your relationship with your possessions might be trying to tell you?

Financial Well-Being

Money wounds shape beliefs and behaviors, often creating extremes in saving, spending, or risk-taking.[23]

Hope's Story

After losing her inheritance in a market crash, Hope moved all her money into low-risk accounts. She knew inflation eroded it, but investing again felt too risky.

At a friend's birthday dinner, casual talk about stocks and dividends got on her nerves: *Doesn't anyone know what could happen?* Later, alone, she wondered: *What if I'm missing something?* She hasn't changed her approach yet, but she bookmarked a beginner article on balanced portfolios. Just seeing it in her browser feels like a crack in the wall.

Healing Tip

Refer to the Window of Tolerance (Chapter 8) to pace your financial exploration to your comfort level.

Connection Question

What small change could you make today to challenge a belief or ease an emotional response that's limiting your financial well-being?

Interconnections: How Adult Financial Trauma Ripples Through Every Part of Life

As we've seen, money wounds don't stay contained. They rarely affect just one part of life. Instead, they ripple outward, touching identity, relationships, work, health, and even spirituality.

Identity and Responsibility: The Adult Trauma Cascade

The eight-dimensional framework validates what trauma survivors often experience but struggle to articulate: that a financial crisis doesn't just affect their bank account. When Malik switched from education to engineering, or when Stella withdrew socially after discovering her spouse's debt, these weren't just financial decisions; they were adaptive responses that touched their core identity and offered a sense of safety.

When money wounds strike in adulthood, they collide with roles and responsibilities. Because adults tend to process financial trauma through the lens of their function as providers, workers, or caregivers, when those roles feel threatened, the impact multiplies.

When Money Betrays Your Expectations

Few shocks hit harder than when financial security doesn't play out the way you thought it would. Hope's inheritance loss shows this breach of trust. It wasn't just about dollars. The loss triggered intellectual barriers (resisting financial education) and emotional upheaval (fear, anxiety, mistrust). When our sense of how the world works gets shattered, the instinct is often to protect ourselves across multiple dimensions at once.

Multiple Entry Points for Healing

The good news is that healing doesn't have to start in one "right" place. For Stella, rebuilding her social connections eased her loneliness and softened financial shame. For Sharon, clearing space in her environment became the doorway to rethinking scarcity. For Mick, revisiting his spiritual practices reshaped his relationship with money.

Any dimension can be a starting point. What matters is movement. Each positive shift creates momentum, carrying into other areas over time.

Charting Your Course: Beyond Financial Trauma

A defining financial event shapes far more than just our money habits. It influences how we think, feel, and act across every dimension of our lives. But these episodes of traumatic stress need not determine your future. Financial resilience isn't focused solely on rebuilding your bank account. It also involves reclaiming your sense of agency and possibility.

The stories in this chapter show that healing often begins with manageable steps in whatever dimension feels most accessible. From there, recovery expands.

Your financial story isn't frozen in the past. With awareness and steady steps, you can move beyond survival mode into a more balanced and empowered relationship with money.

Ready to explore your own financial journey?

Creating Your Personal Wealth Dashboard

To see how financial trauma and healing show up across your life, try building a **personal wealth dashboard**. This visual tool gives you a quick snapshot of where you're thriving and where you may want to focus more attention.

You can download a printable PDF of this dashboard at WholePerson.finance/dashboardPDF. For each dimension (physical, social, etc.), shade the bars from the center outward to reflect your current satisfaction level, from 0% to 100%, based on the following questions. One bar means 10% satisfaction, and ten bars means 100%. Don't overthink it. Go with your gut, not what you think the answer *should* be.

Here are prompts to guide you:

Financial: How confident do you feel about your current money habits and security?

Emotional: How comfortable are you regulating and talking about emotions tied to money?

Intellectual: How satisfied are you with your financial knowledge and decision-making?

Social: How does money influence your relationships with others?

Physical: How well are you maintaining your physical health and energy while managing financial responsibilities?

Spiritual/Existential: How well do your financial choices line up with your deeper values or sense of purpose?

Vocational/Occupational: Does your current job balance financial needs with personal fulfillment?

Environmental: How well does your living space reflect your values and support your well-being?

Personal Wealth Dashboard

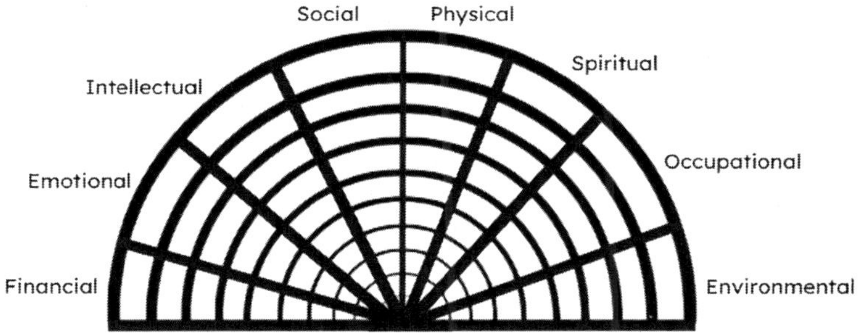

Once you complete your dashboard, pause and reflect. What surprised you? What would you like to release in each area? What would you like to welcome in? What action will you commit to, and why?

As you sit with your personal wealth dashboard, don't just look at each dimension by itself. Notice the connections. Where do your adult responsibilities feel heaviest? Where has life not met your expectations, and what patterns has that created? Most importantly, where can you begin to make changes you'd like to see?

If your dashboard reveals challenges across multiple areas, resist the urge to tackle everything at once. The goal isn't perfection across all dimensions. It's finding one door you're willing to walk through today.

By regularly revisiting this dashboard, you can track your progress and ensure your financial decisions align with a broader vision of wealth: one that's not just about money but about the whole life you're building.

Key Takeaways

- Major financial events impact far more than your bank account; they ripple into your health, work, relationships, spirituality, and other dimensions.
- Many of these effects operate beneath the surface, shaping decisions and behaviors.
- Adverse financial events or circumstances don't have to define you. Recognizing their impact is the first step toward healing.
- Recovery requires a holistic approach that addresses both the numbers and the emotional and nervous system responses beneath them.

You may not have chosen the disruption that started the ripples. But you do have a say in where they flow next. Every small act of healing sends its own ripple through your life and into your future.

The patterns we've traced so far in this book, from childhood origins through adult manifestations, don't unfold in a vacuum. They exist within larger systems that can either amplify or ease financial trauma. Cultural expectations, institutional barriers, media messages, and systemic inequities shape not only what happens to us financially, but how we experience and interpret those events. In the next chapter, we'll zoom out to examine these broader forces and understand how they intersect with our personal stories to create or compound financial trauma.

5

Culture, Systems, and Stigma: The Bigger Picture of Financial Trauma

For many, the words *financial trauma* might immediately suggest personal experiences like eviction or bankruptcy. But the roots of financial trauma reach beyond the individual, embedded deep in the cultural and societal structures that shape our lives.

Earlier chapters showed how trauma reshapes the brain and how childhood and adult experiences leave lasting money patterns. This chapter widens the lens to explore the broader forces behind financial trauma. From systemic inequities to media messaging, these influences can leave deep emotional and financial scars, often invisible yet powerful. Through greater awareness of these forces, you can better understand behaviors that might otherwise remain puzzling.

What You'll Learn in This Chapter

- How systemic factors create and perpetuate financial trauma
- The link between adverse childhood experiences and financial health

- The unique financial challenges marginalized communities face
- How cultural expectations and social media shape our relationship with money
- Strategies for recognizing and responding to the impact of systems on yourself and your money

Beyond Individual Experience: The Systemic Nature of Financial Trauma

Even the most personal money struggles don't unfold in isolation. In this section, we zoom out to examine the larger economic, social, and cultural forces we all must navigate. These systems can either support financial well-being or create conditions where trauma becomes almost inevitable. For communities historically excluded from economic opportunity, particularly Black, Indigenous, and other people of color, these systems haven't just failed to provide support; they've actively produced harm.

To understand how these larger forces generate financial stress, we need to recognize something crucial: These systemic factors aren't self-contained. They layer, intersect, and amplify one another. A person experiencing intergenerational poverty, for instance, might face several compounded challenges at the same time: banking deserts, underfunded schools, and predatory lending. Add discrimination based on race, gender, or other identities, and the weight multiplies further.

What follows isn't a checklist of separate issues but a map of interconnected forces. As you read, notice how one factor often sets the stage for another, creating cascading effects that increase the risk for trauma. Understanding these connections helps explain why individual willpower alone rarely solves financial struggles rooted in systemic inequities.

Systemic Roots of Financial Trauma

Adverse Childhood Experiences

Root Causes

You may have heard of *adverse childhood experiences* (ACEs), the stressful and potentially traumatic events that occur before age 18 such as poverty, abuse, neglect, the lack of a sense of safety at home or in the neighborhood, or parental substance use, incarceration, or domestic violence.

These aren't just bad memories. A large body of research shows ACEs leave a profound and lasting imprint on physical and mental health and shape how we respond to stress throughout our lives.[24]

Although ACEs occur at all income levels, low income is one of the most powerful risk factors for experiencing multiple ACEs.[25] Children in historically marginalized racial and ethnic groups also experience ACEs at higher rates.[26]

Daily Experiences

Not all childhood stress is harmful. But when stressful experiences are severe or chronic or occur without supportive adults to help buffer them, the body's stress response system can remain activated for extended periods. This is called toxic stress, and it's the way ACEs reshape developing brains and bodies.[27] When a child's stress response floods their system with cortisol and other stress hormones day after day, it can disrupt healthy development in ways that persist into adulthood.

Long-Term Effects

Prolonged exposure to stress hormones during critical developmental periods physically reshapes the brain. The emotional alarm center becomes hyperactive and oversensitive to threat, while the connections that help the brain to regulate emotions and think rationally develop more weakly.[28] These types of changes can show up later in adulthood in patterns such as financial avoidance, overspending, or chronic anxiety about money, as explored in Chapter 2.

Lived Experience

Tony grew up watching his stepfather explode over bills. Now Tony's heart races opening his own monthly statements, even though he can afford to pay them. His system still reacts as if financial tasks signal danger.

Tony's emotional alarm center hijacks the moment, while the voice of reason in his brain temporarily shuts down.

Pause + Practice: Even when circumstances improve, your body may still respond as if you're under threat. Try a simple self-compassion practice: Place a hand over your heart and say, *This is hard. And I'm doing the best I can.*

Intergenerational Poverty and Trauma

Root Causes

Systemic barriers such as persistent racial and social discrimination, bias in the criminal justice system, underfunded schools, low wages, banking deserts, and predatory lending practices are powerful forces many families face over generations.

Daily Experiences

These obstacles feed into a cycle where financial struggle feels inescapable.

Long-Term Effects

The research is clear: "Poverty in childhood and among adults can cause poor mental health through social stresses, stigma and trauma."[29] Poverty and trauma aren't separate issues; they're deeply interconnected.

Living under the constant weight of "never enough" breeds hopelessness and despair. Many people cope through self-sabotaging financial behaviors, creating a self-perpetuating cycle.

Lived Experience

Len comes from generations of poverty. He spends money as soon as he gets it, convinced saving is futile. When an unexpected bonus arrives, he splurges on non-essentials. Three weeks later, his car breaks down and he needs a high-interest payday loan. His trauma response, spending right away to avoid the pain of hoping and losing, creates the exact instability he fears.

Pause + Practice: When old patterns pull you toward impulsive choices, pause for three slow breaths. That small space between urge and action is where your power begins.

Len's experience shows how intergenerational patterns, like those we explored in Chapter 3, become magnified when combined with systemic barriers. Len's script, *Saving is pointless because emergencies will always wipe you out,* didn't appear in isolation. It formed through generations of lived experience in systems designed to limit social and economic mobility.

Systemic Discrimination and Financial Exclusion

Root Causes

Systemic inequities within financial and economic institutions have created barriers that disproportionately affect marginalized communities. These discriminatory practices operate across multiple systems at once, creating compounding barriers for Black, Indigenous, people of color, LGBTQ+, older, disabled, and immigrant communities.

Key mechanisms include the historical and ongoing financial industry practices of:

- **Redlining:** denying loans to people in specific geographic areas based on race or ethnicity; now illegal, but its legacy continues
- **Banking deserts:** closing bank branches in inner-city or rural areas
- **Reverse redlining**: charging higher interest rates where competition among financial institutions is low or absent
- **Unequal access to credit** based on identity factors

Broader economic discrimination—through employment, housing, and education—compounds these practices, cutting people off from the foundations needed to build wealth.

Daily Experiences

Many people who are marginalized are pushed into high-cost financial products and excluded from wealth-building opportunities like home equity and small-business loans. The result: lower earnings, higher debt, and limited stability and upward mobility.

Long-Term Effects

These barriers together create a collective sense of disempowerment and distrust of financial systems, making it harder to engage with even the most basic financial services. Financial trauma may emerge from the chronic stress of navigating systems designed to exclude, coupled with a lack of intergenerational wealth transfer and limited access to financial education.

Lived Experiences

- **The Jones Family:** Decades ago, the Joneses, a Black family, were denied a home loan despite qualifying. This rejection scarred them with the belief that building generational wealth through home ownership was unattainable for them. This perspective has shaped financial decisions across generations, creating ongoing cycles of limitation.
- **Rosario:** A refugee from El Salvador with stable income but no U.S. credit history, Rosario has been denied credit again and again. Each rejection reactivates her earlier trauma of poverty and displacement. Her avoidance of banks isn't dysfunction; it's her nervous system shielding her from repeated harm.

These examples show how discrimination takes different forms but creates the same exclusionary patterns across identities.

Issues Affecting Women

Root Causes

Women face unique challenges: unpaid caregiving, parental career disruption, higher rates of financial abuse in relationships (withholding, restricting, or taking money), and wage gaps.

Women working full-time, year-round earn US$0.83 for every US$1.00 earned by men. When part-time and seasonal workers are included, women's earnings drop to $0.78. The gap widens further for women of color, with Black women making about $0.66 and Latina women making about $0.58 for every dollar earned by white, non-Hispanic men.[30] This pay gap cuts across all professions, even those dominated by women.

Daily Experiences

These factors reduce lifetime earnings, savings, and retirement benefits, forcing greater dependence on others or leading to economic vulnerability.

Long-Term Effects

Economic inequality impacts women's mental health. The emotional toll often shows up as higher rates of stress, depression, anxiety, PTSD, eating disorders, and suicide attempts.[31]

After a lifetime of unpaid domestic labor, many women end up with little or no income. Chronic poverty can deepen into traumatic stress.

Lived Experience

Christina left her career to provide family care. Now at retirement age, she lives alone with chronic financial strain. Though her choices were shaped by systemic realities and cultural expectations, she blames herself for her situation.

When Identities Intersect

An immigrant woman of color doesn't face three separate challenges. She faces them simultaneously, each one amplifying the others. The wage gap isn't just about gender or just about race; it's both, compounded by citizenship-based banking exclusion. The nervous system can't distinguish which threat to respond to when they all arrive at once.

Cultural Expectations and Norms

Root Causes

Cultural messages about success, self-worth, and responsibility are powerful.

Cultural norms, especially in wealth-driven economies, often celebrate consumerism and stigmatize financial difficulties, creating a cycle of shame and silence about money problems.

In some cultures, the pressure looks different: less about status display and more about fulfilling collective obligations, such as supporting extended family or sending money home. Either way, cultural standards can create strain.

Daily Experiences

People feel compelled to maintain expectations, even at the cost of overwork, debt, or financial stress. They misread their money struggles as deeply personal failings rather than the product of complex systems.

Long-Term Effects

Tying self-worth to financial status erodes mental health and well-being. It narrows autonomy, fuels anxiety, and entrenches shame.

Lived Experience

Some financial battles unfold behind polished doors, and the people fighting them often feel the most unseen. Nico earns a high income but still lives paycheck to paycheck with no savings. He's maxed out his credit cards and his home equity line trying to keep pace with the lifestyle around him of country clubs, remodels, and the whole performance of success, even though none of it brings him joy. What pulls him in isn't luxury. It's belonging. The impossible tension between social acceptance and financial security keeps him trapped in a pattern of overspending and self-criticism. His debt is now unmanageable, and the fear that his carefully built façade might soon crumble is stirring up old money wounds he thought he'd outgrown.

And while cultural expectations differ across communities, mass communication adds another layer of complexity. In our interconnected world, traditional cultural pressures have been amplified by digital platforms that bring new forms of financial comparison and pressure.

Social Media and Financial Messaging

Root Causes

As a space where millions of users share their best moments, social media creates an illusion of universal prosperity. Many influencers glorify consumer culture and normalize a false reality of extreme lifestyles far beyond most others' reach.

Daily Experiences

The endless scroll of algorithmically tailored, curated messages sparks fear of missing out, relentless comparisons, and feelings of exclusion and inadequacy.

Long-Term Effects

The pressure feeds impulsive spending, debt, and shame. For many, this cycle creates chronic stress which, over time, hardens into financial trauma.

Lived Experience

Lina, burdened with student debt, regularly buys products promoted by her favorite influencers. Each purchase offers a flash of relief from her feelings of inadequacy but deepens her consumer debt and anxiety. Her trauma response, consuming to self-soothe, creates the same instability she fears.

Lina's story shows how modern media supercharges the old "keeping up with the Joneses" pressure. As we saw in Chapter 2, perceived dangers, such as feeling left behind socially or financially, can activate the brain's threat-detection system, interfering with rational money choices.

Taken together, these cultural and systemic forces shape how we feel, think, and act around money, often without us even noticing. But once we start spotting these patterns, we can begin to loosen their grip.

Recognizing Societal Influences in Your Financial Life

Understanding these influences isn't just academic; it's practical. Recognizing these forces can transform how you see your own financial patterns. Awareness reduces shame and opens the door to healing.

But awareness can also spark hard questions like *now what?* The challenge is how to move forward with clarity and courage, even when the system feels stacked against you.

Personal Agency in Navigating Systemic Influences

Beyond Either/Or

Acknowledging systemic influences doesn't erase personal agency. It gives personal agency context. Instead of asking, *Is this problem my fault or the system's?* (a question that fuels shame or helplessness), try asking:

Given the systems I'm navigating, what choices do I have right now?

This shift moves you from blame to empowerment while still honoring real constraints.

You might be feeling the weight of everything we've just explored. Maybe you're thinking: *If all these systems are stacked against me, what's the point of even trying?* Or perhaps the opposite: *Other people face these barriers and succeed. Why can't I just work harder?*

This is the trap that keeps people stuck: feeling powerless or at fault or oscillating between these extremes. One day they blame the system and feel helpless. The next day they blame themselves and feel inadequate or ashamed. Neither extreme leaves room for meaningful action.

What if there was a way to hold both truths at once, acknowledging real barriers while also recognizing where you have power? That's what the following framework offers: a practical tool for sorting what you can control, what you can influence, and what you need to acknowledge but can't change.

The Circles of Influence Model: A Framework for Defining Your Sphere of Influence

When you're dealing with financial trauma, it's easy to feel either stuck or entirely responsible. The Circles of Influence model, popularized by Stephen Covey,[32] helps you find the middle ground: clarifying what you can **control**, what you can **influence**, and what **concern**s you but is outside your control.

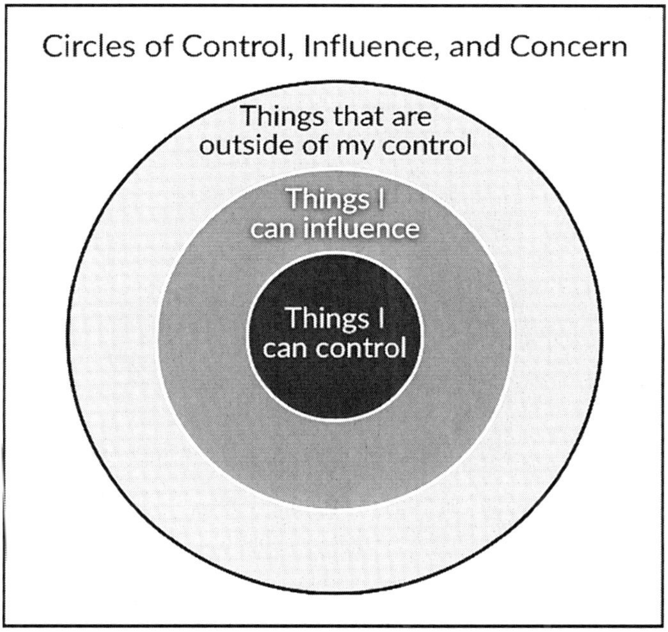

The goal is to shift your focus toward the areas where your decisions have the greatest power to change your financial story.

The table below shows the reach of each circle in your financial life. The examples aren't exhaustive, just enough to get you thinking about where your time and energy go.

Circle	Definition	Examples
Circle of Control	Direct actions and decisions you can make immediately	Spending, saving, and debt repayment choices; mindset and learning habits; noticing trauma responses before making money decisions
Circle of Influence	Areas you can shape but not fully control	Negotiating a raise; improving your credit score; encouraging a partner's good money habits; building trust in a bank despite past betrayals
Circle of Concern	What may matter to you but lies beyond your immediate individual influence	The economy; the stock market; norms and institutions; your family's generational money patterns; discrimination

Systemic inequities may fall within your Circle of Concern as an individual, but they're collective problems that can be addressed through community action, advocacy, and policy change. Recognizing this distinction prevents self-blame while keeping space for shared responsibility.

Here's how this shift in perspective works in practice:

Instead of: *I should be better with money by now.* (shame-based) **Try:** *Given my family's generational financial trauma and the systems I'm working within, what's one small step I can take today in my Circle of Control?* (agency-based)

Instead of: *Everyone else figures money out.* (comparison-based) **Try:** *What barriers in my Circles of Influence and Concern can I name while I work on my Circle of Control?* (reality-based)

Empowerment for Healthy Personal Agency

The myth of the "self-made person" saturates culture. From bootstrap stories in books and movies to curated success posts on social media, the message is the same: *Anyone can succeed through sheer determination.*

What gets erased? Insider connections, family and community support, systemic privilege, and plain luck.

The myth shifts all responsibility to the individual, so when success doesn't come, shame rushes in.[33]

Watch for signs that misplaced responsibility has slipped into shame in your story:

- You dismiss real barriers you face.
- You compare your inner struggles to others' outer appearances.

Instead, when facing financial challenges, here's what you can do:

1. **Notice systemic factors that may be shaping the situation** (provides context).
2. **Name what you can influence** within your Circles of Control and Influence (identifies possibilities).
3. **Choose one manageable action** that recognizes both your barriers and your power (keeps it doable).
4. **Seek support** from people, resources, or practices that help you move forward (prevents isolation).
5. **Practice self-compassion** as you repeat this process and navigate your finances (relieves shame, maintains emotional safety).

This framework validates your reality while still empowering you to act. Not in idealized circumstances but in your actual life.

Example in Practice

Daryna's Story: Daryna immigrated to the U.S. three years ago. She works full-time, pays rent on time, and manages her expenses carefully. But when she applied for a small car loan, she was denied. Not because of poor credit, but because she had no credit history at all. Each rejection felt like a verdict on her worth, echoing old messages that she'd never belong or be trusted with opportunity.

Shame-based approach: *Everyone says I should build good credit, but even when I work hard and pay on time, I fail. I must be doing something wrong. Maybe I'm just not responsible enough.*

Systemic awareness + personal agency approach: *When I met with a credit counselor at the neighborhood center today, I found out the system isn't neutral. It was built for people who already have access to credit, not for those like me starting from scratch. But there are still things within my control. I can open a secured credit card, ask a friend to add me as an authorized user, and use a rent-reporting service to build a credit history. I may have to wait a while longer to get a car, but now I see a clear path forward.*

Reflection Questions: Identifying Systemic Factors

These questions invite you to notice how larger forces may have shaped your financial experiences. Try journaling about them or discussing them with a trusted person. The aim isn't to solve everything at once but to build awareness.

Beyond your immediate family, how did your childhood environment (neighborhood, community resources, local economy) shape your early understanding of money?

How have your cultural and demographic identities affected your access to financial opportunities?

What cultural money messages do you carry?

How does social media affect your financial self-image?

What institutional barriers have you encountered financially?

The insights you discover will provide understanding, but actions are what transform them into real-life impact. Let's get started now.

Taking Action: First Steps

Here are two simple ways to begin. Choose what feels right for you.

1. **Audit your media diet.** Notice what platform or content sparks a sense of financial inadequacy. Delete, mute, or unfollow it.
2. **Challenge internalized messages:** When you hear thoughts like *I should have more by now,* or *Everyone else has this figured out,* pause. Ask yourself where these expectations come from and whether they align with reality.

Breaking the Cycle: Moving Forward

Cultural and societal forces don't just shape how we manage money. They shape how we *feel* about it. Recognizing these influences helps separate your self-worth from circumstances you didn't choose.

This broader perspective doesn't remove personal responsibility but contextualizes it. You can hold yourself accountable while also honoring the barriers you face. Often, money behaviors, even those that at first seem counterproductive, make sense when seen as adaptive responses to overwhelming conditions.

This path from awareness to healing isn't straight, and it unfolds differently for everyone. It often moves like a river: sometimes rushing, sometimes barely flowing, yet always finding its way forward.

Key Takeaways

- Financial trauma often stems from systemic inequities and intergenerational patterns.
- Marginalized communities carry compounded burdens that increase vulnerability.
- Cultural money taboos fuel silence and shame.
- Social media and wealth messaging reinforce harmful comparisons.
- Awareness of these influences reduces shame and creates space for healing.

The systemic, cultural, and generational forces we explored in this chapter don't remain distant or theoretical. They become personal. What starts as discrimination in lending practices or pay inequities becomes the voice in your head that whispers *people like me don't deserve financial security*. What begins as cultural pressure to maintain appearances becomes the shame that floods in when you can't. What originates in generational poverty becomes the belief that you're inherently broken with money.

This is how systems get under our skin: not usually through one dramatic event, but through a thousand small moments that eventually tell us a story about who we are. And once that story takes hold, it doesn't just sit quietly. It creates its own destructive momentum, a cycle that can feel impossible to escape.

Understanding these broader contexts helps us see our struggles with compassion. But it also reveals something crucial: We can't recover from financial trauma without addressing the shame that gives it staying power. While we can't always change the systems around us, we can interrupt how they operate within us. That's where the next chapter takes us: into the anatomy of shame itself, and the practical exit ramps that can help us break free.

6

The Cycle of Shame

Financial trauma leaves a raw wound; shame is our story of what that wound says about who we are.

Millions of people silently carry money trauma. Over two-thirds of Americans report experiencing it.[34] What's rarely discussed is how trauma intertwines with shame. This chapter explores that connection and how to break free.

What You'll Learn in This Chapter

- How financial adversity, inadequacy, acute shame, and self-defeating behaviors form a self-reinforcing cycle
- How external forces intensify the pressures within the cycle
- How exit ramps are available for breaking free at every stage
- How to use practical tools to reframe beliefs and rebuild confidence

The Cycle: How Financial Struggle Becomes Identity Wound

The **Cycle of Financial Trauma and Shame** is a model I created to help visualize the complex relationship between financial trauma and shame.

At its core, the cycle has four parts:

- Negative financial circumstances
- A sense of personal inadequacy
- Acute shame
- Behavioral and health issues

Each part feeds the others, creating a loop that can be hard to escape. But each also offers an "exit ramp" to slow or break the cycle.

Here's how the pieces fit together visually:

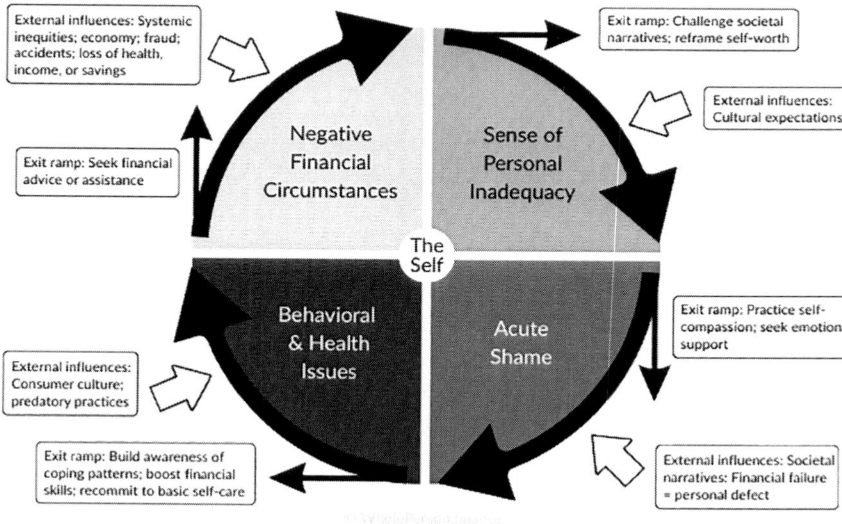

The Cycle of Financial Trauma and Shame and the Exit Ramps That Break It

Breaking out of the cycle is tricky. Trauma makes change feel risky, and systemic barriers can slow progress. Some people face bigger obstacles than others. But with awareness, self-kindness, and persistence, exiting is possible.

This cycle isn't just a concept. It's lived experience. Let's explore what it can feel like from the inside.

Rhea's Story

Rhea, a 35-year-old teacher, carries both medical bills and student debt. She compares herself to others who seem better off and feels her struggles mean she's less competent or not trying hard enough. To conceal her financial and perceived personal limitations, she withdraws from friends and colleagues. She develops headaches and sleep problems from chronic stress. These health problems affect her work performance, jeopardizing her much-needed income. She's caught in the cycle of shame.

Rhea's experience reflects a common pattern. Money problems don't stop at the numbers on a bill. They tangle with our sense of adequacy, self-worth, and health, fueling a vicious cycle that feels impossible to escape. Like a wheel in motion, one element drives the next, sustained by external pressures and reinforced by our own patterns.

Her story shows how financial struggles and shame seep into multiple areas of life. But how does that happen? Let's break the cycle down, one part at a time, and explore how we can disrupt it.

Negative Financial Circumstances

Negative financial circumstances are difficulties that strain our resources or threaten our stability. They can come from acute or chronic causes during childhood or adulthood. The roots might go back many years.

How They Fuel the Cycle

When exploring the role of these negative circumstances, it's tempting to focus on personal choice, like taking on too much debt. But our financial lives unfold within a web of external forces, many of which are beyond our control.

These external factors, from systemic inequities to problems in the economy, can take a toll on our personal financial outcomes. And society's messaging about financial setbacks being a "personal failure" adds a layer of shame.[35]

Understanding this broader context helps explain why negative financial circumstances so often feel overwhelming and insurmountable. But knowing you're not alone in facing forces beyond your control can take some of the pressure off. Money challenges are not failure; they're part of a system that's stacked in ways that make things harder for many people.

The Impact on the Self

Financial adversity creates stress and instability. Negative financial circumstances or the situations they lead to, such as eviction, can feed into feelings of personal inadequacy (*I should be doing better,* or *I should have been able to prevent this problem*).

When we start seeing ourselves as fundamentally "not good enough," we feel shame. Shame doesn't just result from specific circumstances. It colors how we experience them, making them feel more devastating or permanent. Over time, this can create long-lasting negative beliefs about ourselves. These beliefs become part of our core identity and persist across different situations, not just financial ones.[36]

Once shame takes hold, it doesn't just sit quietly in the background. It starts to influence how we behave, especially when we feel exposed or vulnerable. Shame makes it more difficult to take the actions necessary to move beyond our negative financial circumstances. The good side? Awareness of these patterns is powerful. Noticing how shame shows up is the first step toward stepping out of its grip.

How Shame Shows Up

- **Avoidance Response:** Shame drives withdrawal. We may cling to familiar but difficult circumstances rather than risk failure in better ones. Or we convince ourselves we don't belong in improved situations at all.
- **Social Disconnection:** Besides avoidance, shame breeds isolation.[37] We avoid professional contacts, feel like impostors in education or work settings, or withdraw from spaces that seem "not for people like me."
- **Biological Stress Response:** The body reacts to shame as if to physical danger.[38] For people with financial trauma, this may mean anxiety symptoms when facing advancement opportunities, stress in unfamiliar settings, or a sense that the body's reaction confirms not belonging.

This tangle of negative circumstances and shame hinders financial well-being in ways that go beyond practical limitations.

Jamal's Story: The Ripple Effects of an Unexpected Expense

When Jamal's car broke down, the $1,800 repair bill shattered his careful budget. Time off work due to the sudden breakdown meant lost income. Late fees piled up as he struggled to catch up, and his credit score fell. He began to wonder what was wrong with him to be in this situation, and the stress took a toll on his health, adding doctor's bills and more time off work. Even though he was trying his hardest, Jamal felt like he was sinking, as negative circumstances magnified one another.

The Compound Effect

Money problems seldom stay contained. One crisis sparks another. Jamal's repair bill led to late fees, damaged credit, lost wages, health issues, and higher costs in the future. A single setback snowballed into a cascade of new obstacles.

That's why recovery often feels impossible. The challenge becomes not just solving the original problem but stopping the chain reaction it sets in motion.

Recognizing this effect doesn't mean giving up. It means breaking the chain.

External support systems, whether family resources, workplace flexibility, or community assistance, can be the difference between a temporary detour and a long-term spiral. Without those safety nets, every financial challenge can feel existential, activating the nervous system's alarms and clouding clear thinking.

Reflection Prompts

What external factors have impacted your financial circumstances? How could they be affecting your life today? How might you be able to set up safeguards against future challenges, no matter how slowly?

The Exit Ramp: Finding Your Way Forward

- **Seek practical tools and support.** Even small acts, like calling a credit counselor or asking about payment plans, reduce overwhelm.
- **Build skills gradually.** Focus on one area at a time, such as learning strategies to improve your credit score or exploring affordable insurance.
- **Connect with others.** Finding people who share similar struggles reminds you you're not alone.

Even when challenges feel stacked against you, actions matter. Each effort, no matter how tiny, builds new pathways, momentum, and resilience.

Financial strain doesn't just stress our wallets. Over time, it reshapes how we see ourselves. That's where the next part of the cycle begins.

A Sense of Personal Inadequacy

Inadequacy whispers, "You're not enough." Social comparisons and others' expectations can amplify this voice until it's deafening. But hearing the whisper doesn't mean it's true. You can learn to recognize it and respond with curiosity and self-compassion instead of acceptance.

How External Pressures Contribute

As explored in Chapter 5, we're bombarded with cultural scripts about what "successful" people should achieve at certain stages of life: home ownership, career advancement, retirement savings. Social media intensifies the pressure with carefully curated messaging. Family expectations and generational patterns add more weight, while societal myths about meritocracy tell us that if we struggle, it must be our fault.

These pressures don't stay abstract. They show up in daily life: in casual conversations about vacations or big purchases, in job interviews where we're asked to share our five-year plan, and in social gatherings where success is tallied in achievements and acquisitions. Over time, these influences seep into identity, making inadequacy feel deeply rooted. Even so, identity isn't fixed. Noticing these pressures gives you the power to question them and choose which voices guide your sense of self.

The Impact on the Self

This sense of inadequacy doesn't sit passively in the background. It actively shapes behavior in ways that can worsen financial circumstances. When you believe you're unsuccessful or unable to manage money, you might:

- Avoid financial education, thinking *people like me don't invest.*
- Accept lower-paying positions because you don't believe you deserve better.
- Procrastinate on financial decisions, assuming you'll make the wrong choice.
- Dismiss wins as luck rather than skill, preventing you from identifying your abilities and building on your success.

The Inner Critic's Financial Voice

Inadequacy often speaks through a persistent inner critic that provides running commentary on our financial lives. It whispers: *You're 40 and still renting. What's wrong with you?* or *Everyone else has their retirement figured out but you.*

The inner critic's voice is different from healthy self-reflection. The inner critic operates from a place of comparison and judgment rather than growth and learning. It becomes especially loud during transitions or setbacks, transforming neutral circumstances into personal indictments. Under its influence, clear decision-making becomes almost impossible.

Remember: The inner critic is a personality mode, not a prophecy. Naming it and noticing when it speaks creates space to break free from its influence.

Michael's Story: Hidden Fears

When his company announces layoffs, Michael loses his job. Panic sets in. Instead of reaching out for leads or applying for new roles, he shuts down. Doubt floods in: *What if I've lost my edge in the job market? What if I'm rejected again?*

He lingers in unemployment, unable to see his past successes or recognize the value he brings. The fear of being confirmed as inadequate outweighs his desire to act.

Michael's experience is common, but it doesn't define him. Awareness of these patterns is the first step toward reclaiming agency, and even small movement on the exit ramp can loosen the grip of inadequacy.

Reflection Prompts

What messages have you internalized about financial success, and how do they shape your self-perception? When have feelings of inadequacy held you back from an opportunity? What new perspective might free you?

The Exit Ramp: A Path to Self-Acceptance

- **Redefine success.** Question cultural standards and create success metrics grounded in your own values.
- **Name your strengths.** Keep a list of your skills, wins, and character traits as evidence against self-doubt.
- **Seek support.** Surround yourself with people who value you for who you are, not what you achieve.

These strategies won't erase a sense of inadequacy overnight, but over time they'll build resilience, confidence, and a more balanced sense of self.

Inadequacy sets the stage for a much deeper emotional experience: shame. Shame goes beyond feeling like we've made a mistake or fallen short of expectations. It convinces us that we, as individuals, are inherently flawed or unworthy.

The progression from inadequacy to shame is a critical escalation. Inadequacy whispers, "You're not good enough at this particular thing." Shame roars, "You're not good enough, period." This shift from narrow self-criticism to sweeping self-condemnation is what makes shame so corrosive and so much harder to recover from.

Let's dive deeper into this dynamic.

Acute Shame

Acute Shame versus Chronic Shame

It's important to distinguish between acute shame, the focus of this section, and the chronic shame that runs through every part of the cycle.

Acute shame is the lightning strike. It hits suddenly, crystallizing vague unease into identity-level beliefs. Chronic shame is the storm that lingers, saturating everything. It becomes the emotional atmosphere, making the entire cycle more toxic.

Chronic shame intensifies the impact of every quadrant of the shame cycle model. It makes **financial circumstances** feel catastrophic, **inadequacy** feel permanent, and **behavioral responses** feel more extreme. It transforms external events into internal character judgments. Shame may not be the only player in the cycle, but it's the psychological glue that holds it all together.

When Shame Takes Hold

Shame appears in many painful ways: harsh self-criticism, hyper-awareness of others' opinions, or an overwhelming urge to hide.

Acute shame is often the point in the cycle where things feel most stuck. It makes reaching out for help or trying something new feel incredibly vulnerable.

When money problems hit, shame doesn't just sting. It sears itself into our self-image. A past due payment isn't just a missed deadline. It's proof, we think, that we're broken.

Soon, we start to view ourselves as fundamentally deficient. The belief settles in that our own inadequacy is to blame for our struggles.

Where External Pressure Comes From

Shame is an insidious emotion that twists external events into character judgments, often in a way that's overly critical and debilitating. Consider unmanageable debt:

External event: Negotiating with creditors over a massive balance.

Shame-driven character judgment: *I'm a failure. I'll never be able to manage my finances. I'm so irresponsible for ending up here.*

From this scenario we can see that attributing financial problems to personal defects can be damaging, as it:

- **Overgeneralizes:** One setback becomes a defining characteristic.
- **Ignores context:** Many external factors, such as unexpected expenses or a sudden change in income, might have contributed to the situation.
- **Keeps us stuck:** There's no room for learning and growth if failures come from fixed limitations.

Seeing how shame twists external events into self-condemnation allows you to separate shame's narrative from reality. One overdue payment doesn't define you. It's just a number, not a measure of your worth.

How Shame Fuels the Cycle

Financial trauma leaves a raw wound; shame is our story of what that wound says about who we are. Here are some ways in which this happens.

Concealment

Unlike trauma's protection responses (fight, flight, freeze, fawn), shame creates concealment responses. When we experience financial shame, we don't just react to external threats; we try to cover up evidence of our perceived defectiveness.[39]

We do this through hiding or secrecy, when we conceal the source of shame out of fear of judgment. Or we cover up shame through denial, when we downplay, rationalize, or outright reject "shameful" events.[40]

Isolation

Shame whispers that it's safer to disappear than risk exposure. We withdraw socially to avoid judgment or rejection. We skip events we can't afford or decline professional opportunities that might expose our financial situation.

Global Self-Condemnation

Shame expands until it covers everything. What begins as *I overspent this month* can quickly spiral into *I'm irresponsible with money* and finally *I'm a failure as an adult.*

Time Fusion

Shame collapses time, making past or present setbacks feel like permanent prophecies. A financial setback "proves" things won't change as time passes, eliminating hope and motivation: *I'm 45 and still living paycheck to paycheck* becomes *I'll never get ahead.*

Performance = Worth

Shame convinces us our financial performance equals our value as human beings. Net worth becomes self-worth, feeding a harsh internal narrative: *My low credit score proves I'm a complete failure. I'm worthless.*

Even when shame spreads in this way, noticing the pattern is the first step toward reclaiming perspective. You can learn to pause before accepting its messages.

Milla's Money Story

As a child, Milla watched her family lose everything after her father's illness led to bankruptcy. Many years later, she still remembers neighbors whispering, her parents' hushed conversations about being "failures," a box of second-hand children's clothes left anonymously on the doorstep.

Today, every financial setback awakens that old shame. The story rushes back: She's destined to repeat the past; it's in her DNA.

Milla's experience isn't unique. Many of us inherit unspoken financial shame and carry it forward like an old debt we never signed up for. But remember this: Inherited shame may feel like a permanent shadow, but it can be chased away by light. Understanding its origin gives you the tools to change your relationship with money and redefine your self-worth.

Reflection Prompts

What emotions and physical sensations surface when you imagine asking for help or sharing your struggles? Instead of pushing them away, try asking: How might they be trying to protect me? What are they trying to tell me?

The Exit Ramp: A Path to Safety, Self-Worth, and Connection

Breaking out of the shame cycle, especially in the acute shame quadrant, isn't a matter of thinking positively or toughening up. It takes small, intentional measures: self-kindness, courage to reach out, and a trauma-aware approach. Each act chips away at shame's grip.

- **Practice self-compassion.** Financial challenges don't define self-worth. Shift the script from *I'm a loser* to *I made the best choice I could with what I knew. I'm learning, and next time might look different.* Try this: Write down a recent money issue that unsettled you, then respond with the same kindness you'd offer a close friend.
- **Disrupt isolation.** Shame thrives in silence. Whether it's hearing "I've been there too" or receiving guidance tailored to your needs, connection can dissolve shame.
- **Address the deep shame and physical stress response.** A trauma-aware approach explores root causes, reframes harmful beliefs, and introduces body-based tools to support long-term nervous system healing.

Shame doesn't just change how we think or feel. It changes what we *do*. And too often, the ways we cope end up digging the hole deeper, eroding not just our finances, but our mental and physical health.

Behavioral and Health Issues

What makes this stage of the shame cycle uniquely challenging is that behaviors are often confused with the underlying problem. Because behaviors are external, they're more noticeable than internal states. So we tend to focus on curbing behaviors such as overspending, avoidance, or stress-shopping, without recognizing they're symptoms of deeper wounds.[41]

Chronic shame makes us judge these coping behaviors more harshly, adding another layer of self-criticism to an already difficult situation. And let's be honest: Popular culture piles on. Some media personalities and bestselling authors have built careers by scolding and berating people in financial crisis, turning human pain into a spectacle. When that voice gets repeated enough, it seeps into our own inner dialogue, convincing us we deserve the shame we carry.

But when we understand behavior patterns as adaptive responses to trauma and shame rather than unrelated actions, we can begin to address them with self-empathy and effectiveness. This shift in perspective opens the door to viewing challenges with curiosity instead of judgment, and to taking steps that actually help.

How the Cycle Keeps Going

Consumer culture and predatory lenders don't just wait for us to stumble. They shove. They feed on shame, offering quick fixes and hollow promises of worth. In moments of vulnerability, we become easy prey for marketing that sells status or escape.[42]

The cycle is further complicated by healthcare access. Mental health support, sometimes crucial for breaking patterns of financial trauma and shame, remains limited or unaffordable for many. And physical health issues, whether caused by financial stress or worsened by delayed care, can spiral into new crises through medical bills and lost work hours. This creates a devastating feedback loop of worsening health and financial instability.

When mental or physical challenges spike, coping behaviors surge.[43] These might take the form of impulsive or compulsive spending or disengagement from real-world money concerns. Trauma and shame hide beneath them all, eroding long-term stability. Noticing these patterns is the first step toward change. Awareness gives you the chance to intervene before the cycle escalates.

Common Behavioral Patterns

As we saw in Chapter 2, trauma responses often follow predictable patterns: **avoidance behaviors** such as unopened bills, **hypervigilance** like hoarding money even when spending is appropriate, and **emotional soothing** such as shopping binges after stress or loss.

Internal and external forces can create shame over these behaviors.

And as we'll explore in Chapter 10, the fallout of shame shows up in relationships, too. We see it behaviors such as **secrecy about money**, **difficulty accepting help**, or **conflicts over spending** that stem from deep shame rather than practical disagreements.

Seeing these patterns in ourselves isn't a mark of weakness. It's information. Each insight is a tool you can use to make different choices next time.

The Toll on Health

Chronic stress, including financial stress, embeds itself in our bodies, minds, and behaviors. It shows up physically through sleep disruption, elevated cortisol levels, weakened immune function, and increased inflammation. It also increases the risk of cardiovascular disease and accidents. Many people report symptoms like headaches, digestive issues, or muscle tension that correlate directly with their financial stress levels.[44]

We experience financial trauma in ways that mirror physical danger, triggering the same stress hormones that would activate during threats to our survival. The body registers each instance. And it sends the bill.

Sleep loss is especially destructive. One in three people report that financial stress negatively affects their sleep, with almost one in four of these experiencing severe issues like nightmares, insomnia, and fatigue.[45] When we can't sleep, we can't think clearly. Exhaustion hijacks our decisions.

Meanwhile, disordered financial behaviors emerge as attempts to cope with shame and trauma. These might include taking on high-interest debt, gambling excessively, or self-sabotaging our income or savings.

Each financially destructive act reinforces shame's lies: *I am broken. I am worthless.* The very actions taken to escape the pain of the trauma-shame cycle often deepen financial difficulties.

Orlando's experience shows how these health and behavioral responses can create their own destructive momentum.

Orlando's Story: When Coping Behaviors Create New Problems

For years, Orlando coped with his shame over a low income by buying small luxuries he couldn't afford. A new gadget or night out felt like an antidote. But the credit card bills mounted, and the shame grew.

As his problems intensified, so did his avoidance behaviors. He drank more to dull the anxiety, but this impaired his judgment and health. When an unexpected medical bill arrived, it was the tipping point.

Sleepless nights kicked in, driven by his stress response. At work, fatigue eroded his focus and performance. That sparked fresh anxiety about losing his job and his much-needed income.

Orlando felt caught in a trap, unsure of how to break free. His self-sabotaging coping behaviors had become a prison.

Orlando's story feels intense, but it's not a life sentence. Understanding the connection between behavior, stress, and shame gives him—and all of us—the power to start making manageable, effective changes.

Reflection Prompts

Do you turn to any behaviors when financial stress rises? How do they affect your health and overall well-being?

The Exit Ramp: Action Steps to Financial Recovery

Escaping the shame cycle in the health and behavior quadrant starts with awareness and builds through small, gutsy moves toward growth and learning:

- Notice your go-to coping patterns without judgment.
- Focus on what you can control.
- Enlist professional support as needed.
- Approach new financial skills with curiosity.
- Recommit to basic self-care: sleep, food, movement, connection, and health care.

Even micro-actions begin to tilt the balance in your favor. These include steps like paying one bill, getting one good night of sleep, or making one careful decision. The smallest action matters. More than you think. Because those actions don't just stop the cycle. They start a new one.

Breaking Free from Shame: Writing a New Money Story

As we've seen, the cycle of financial trauma and shame is complex, with many contributing factors. But at every stage of the cycle lies an exit ramp: a chance to shift direction and begin a new story.

As early actions start to add up, self-belief grows. That's how an upward spiral takes off.

This process isn't neat or linear. It's recursive. You might find yourself revisiting certain stages over and over, each time peeling back another layer. The goal isn't perfection. It's a deepening of understanding, agency, and self-compassion.

Most importantly, you discover a new narrative: Your past or present struggles do not dictate your future. In this story, your worth is innate, unconditional, and unshakeable.

Wherever you are in this cycle, know this: You're not alone, you're not to blame, and change is possible. Your financial history is part of your story, but it's not the whole story. You are more than your bank balance, your credit score, or your hardest moments.

You're a person of inherent worth, deserving dignity, security, and joy. Your story isn't finished. And you hold the pen.

Key Takeaways

- Financial trauma creates a self-reinforcing loop: adversity → inadequacy → shame → harmful behaviors → back to adversity.
- External forces shape financial realities, shattering the myth that money struggles are purely individual failures.
- Acute shame attacks identity, making it the most toxic element in the cycle.
- Trauma responses make sense; they once kept you safe.
- Exit ramps exist at every stage. Wherever you find traction, you can interrupt the cycle.

If you carry only one thing forward, let it be this: The cycle may be strong, but it's not stronger than you.

The shame that tells us we're broken can drive us to behaviors that reinforce that very belief. We might sabotage our own financial stability, unconsciously confirming our deepest fears about our unworthiness.

These destructive actions are not a sign of personal failing; they are a manifestation of our trauma responses. But over time, these responses can become ingrained as **self-defeating patterns.**

In the next chapter, we'll explore how financial trauma drives us to work against our own best interests, and more importantly, how to recognize these patterns and develop the tools to support ourselves instead of sabotaging our progress. Because healing doesn't stop at understanding what happened to us. It also means reclaiming our power to choose what happens next.

7

Self-Sabotage: Why We Undermine Our Own Financial Well-Being

Do you ever find yourself undermining your own financial progress? Maybe you save diligently, then spend it all in one impulsive moment. You commit to paying down debt, but something inside resists. Or you let bills pile up, even when you have enough money to pay them.

Part of you feels in control, yet another part seems guided by an invisible force. No matter how hard you try, your financial reality doesn't match your vision.

That's self-sabotage. It's not a lack of discipline or an inability to follow through. It's driven by hidden beliefs and trauma responses shaped by past experiences. Awareness of this link is the key to breaking the cycle and creating the stability you want.

I saw this in my own journey. At one time, when money felt overwhelming, I'd either act impulsively or avoid it altogether. But when I realized these behaviors weren't the result of permanent deficits but of learned responses, I was able to start making small movements toward lasting change.

This chapter will help you uncover hidden ties between your money wounds and self-sabotaging routines so that you can understand your patterns, reshape them, and take back control of your financial future.

What You'll Learn in This Chapter

- Why trauma-based financial self-sabotage isn't about willpower but about thought patterns, emotions, and nervous system responses
- How to spot your own self-sabotaging patterns
- Why recognition is the key to breaking the cycle for good
- Practical ways to turn self-sabotaging patterns into behaviors that support your goals

How Financial Trauma Leads to Self-Sabotage

Financial wounds that cause severe or chronic stress can leave lasting marks on your relationship with money. Maybe you grew up in a household scraping by, where conflict over money was constant. Or perhaps you faced your own crisis of long-term unemployment, crushing debt, business losses, or a costly legal battle.

These experiences don't simply fade, even if you rarely think about them. They live on in ingrained trauma responses and unconscious beliefs that once served to protect you.

Self-sabotage is one of these protective patterns. It exists to shield you from danger. If you once endured a sudden financial loss, your brain may link accumulating savings with the fear of losing them again. Or if you grew up in financial chaos, you may unconsciously recreate it in adulthood because order feels abnormal.

The Protective Origin of Self-Sabotage

The brain's threat-response system works like a protective alarm system (see Chapter 2). In a crisis, this alarm system kicks in. Your body reacts with fight, flight, freeze, or fawn, exactly as designed.

But the problem is, after the danger passes, the system can get stuck. It continues to blare, even with no threat in sight. It can't tell past danger from present opportunity.

That's where self-sabotage comes in. To protect you from a future threat, your brain steers you back into familiar, even painful, territory. For example:

- **Fear of Success**: If past success brought criticism or abuse, your brain may now equate success with danger. To avoid a repeat, your brain may opt for procrastinating or for quitting just before the finish line.
- **Fear of Having Money**: If money once fueled interpersonal problems, such as fights, manipulation, or demands from relatives, your brain may link money with loss or painful emotions. As your income or savings grow, your brain may trigger overspending or impulse shopping to get rid of the money and neutralize the threat.

The core idea is that self-sabotage isn't an inability to persevere or a desire to fail. It's a deeply ingrained survival strategy that once served a purpose. By understanding this, we can begin to address the underlying trauma rather than only the behavior. You can't just tell the alarm to turn off. You have to teach the nervous system that it's finally safe to stand down.

The Safety Paradox

Even when we understand that trauma responses have a protective origin, their self-sabotaging effects can still be baffling. A system designed to help us ends up hurting us instead.

The nervous system leans toward caution: It's better to set off a multitude of false alarms than to fail to alert you to that one true hazard. But living in constant high alert hijacks clear thinking about money, pulling you toward patterns of self-sabotage. Understanding that this is a primitive brain response, not a personal failing, is key in regaining control.

Recognition of Self-Sabotage

Unaddressed financial trauma often shows up as patterns that quietly erode both your money and well-being. Here are a few examples:

- Avoidance: Ignoring bills, avoiding budgets, or refusing to check your bank account can feel safer than facing reality, even though the delay only makes things worse.
- Impulsive Spending: This may bring a quick rush of relief or joy, but it often ends in regret and deepens shame over money decisions.
- Under-earning: You might avoid pursuing raises or higher-paying roles, even when peers with similar qualifications move ahead.

These behaviors clash with your conscious goals, but they're driven by unconscious nervous system patterns. Under stress, the brain grabs quick shortcuts. They're useful in crisis but damaging when old threats spill into today's financial life.

The Thinking Patterns Behind Self-Sabotage

Self-sabotaging behaviors are often fueled by specific thought patterns called cognitive distortions that can emerge when your nervous system is in a protective mode.[46]

In this mode, the brain skips nuance. It craves fast, decisive shortcuts to keep you safe. These thinking patterns make perfect sense during actual threats, but they become problematic when, because of trauma, your nervous system can't tell past danger from present safety (see Chapter 2).

Learning how these patterns work gives you a clear way to spot when your protective system has taken over. Instead of wondering, *why am I doing this?* you can name the mental pathway driving your behavior. Let's look at the most common ones and how they play out in real financial lives.

All-or-Nothing Thinking

This distortion sees finances in extremes: total control or utter failure, complete success or inevitable ruin. All-or-nothing thinking often traces back to nervous system reactions during truly extreme moments where safety or danger were the only options, with no middle ground. In those moments, black-and-white thinking was protective because it helped us make quick survival decisions without getting lost in nuance.

For example, someone who unconsciously believes that having money means losing it might reason, *If I save, I'll just lose it anyway, so why bother?* That belief fuels avoidance of saving or investing, creating the very instability they dread.

Harper's Story: When Harper received a tax refund, she considered starting an emergency fund. But childhood memories of her parents losing everything surged back. Her child brain had learned there's either total security or none. She spent the refund on impulse buys, reinforcing the instability she longed to escape. This outcome wasn't from a lack of discipline. Her brain's security system was shielding her from a repeat of a painful experience.

Overgeneralization

Overgeneralization happens when we draw sweeping conclusions from a single setback. One failed investment or financial loss gets translated into: *Every time I have money, I lose it.* This thought pattern develops as a protective mechanism when the nervous system endures a catastrophic loss or when we're so vulnerable we can't risk another mistake. The brain treats one bad outcome as proof that all similar situations are dangerous. To protect us, it steers us away from whole categories of risk.

This response often fuels self-sabotage, either by avoiding taking financial actions altogether or by overlooking opportunities, convinced any gain will vanish as it did once in the past.

Ravi's Story: When Ravi lost most of his assets in the stock market, he concluded, *I'm terrible with money.* Years later, a friend invited him to join an investment club. He dismissed it immediately: *Investments never work out for me.* His nervous system had overgeneralized from one painful event, trying to protect him from vulnerability. Instead, it blocked him from exploring both financial growth and community.

Mental Filtering

Mental filtering fixates on the negative while dismissing the positive. We spotlight mistakes and overlook wins until financial stability feels out of reach. This often develops when our nervous system learns that missing a threat could be dangerous. If we grew up in a financially unstable home where ignoring a bill or being "too optimistic" led to crisis, our brain adapted by scanning constantly for what could go wrong.

At first, this vigilance feels protective. But over time, it narrows our focus to only risks and failures. That constant scanning heightens anxiety, which can eventually tip into avoidance: ignoring bills, delaying decisions, or giving up entirely. What began as self-protection ends up creating the very instability we're desperate to avoid.

Sofia's Story: Sofia paid off her car loan and built a solid credit score, but she couldn't see those wins. Her brain filtered them out, highlighting only what remained: the credit card debt. As a child, she'd watched her parents lose their small business after missing warning signs, so her brain learned to scan for danger constantly. But this hypervigilance backfired. The constant focus on what was wrong heightened her anxiety until checking her statements felt unbearable. She began avoiding bills entirely. What started as protective vigilance ended up fueling the financial chaos she feared.

Catastrophizing

Catastrophizing is imagining the worst possible outcome even if it's unlikely. For someone with financial trauma, it can make any financial risk feel like certain ruin. This thought pattern emerges when the nervous system has witnessed sudden financial disasters, such as job loss, medical bills, market crashes, or family crises. The brain learns to anticipate worst-case scenarios as a way to mentally prepare for and potentially prevent devastating outcomes.

This fear of a negative outcome can trigger self-sabotage through extreme risk aversion that prevents wealth-building, or even through reckless financial behavior since *It's all going to fall apart sooner or later anyway.*

Eli's Story: When Eli thought about asking for a raise, his heart raced and he imagined disaster: *My boss will say no, think I'm ungrateful, and fire me.* When he was young, his father's sudden job loss had trained Eli's brain to expect the worst possible outcome. Now, Eli's protective responses stopped him from discussing a raise. This saved him from imagined ruin but quietly sabotaged his long-term earnings, undermining the financial security he yearned for.

"Should" Statements

"Should" statements are self-criticisms using *should, must*, or *ought*. With money, it looks like: *I should have figured this out by now* or *I must never make financial mistakes.* These rigid rules often form when the nervous system learned that financial errors carried serious consequences like harsh criticism, anger, or loss of safety. "Should" statements are attempts to avoid emotional or relational danger, but the standards they set are impossible to meet.

When reality falls short, these standards breed guilt, shame, and a sense of inadequacy. The result? Avoidance of tasks or abandonment of goals because perfection feels out of reach.

Kay's Story: Kay grew up hearing that adults should know how to manage money. Mistakes meant failure, not learning. Now at 27, she berated herself for budgeting struggles: *I should be better at this!* Shame drove her to avoid bills altogether. Her nervous system was trying to protect her from the criticism she'd learned to associate with financial struggles, but the unrealistic standards created more of the very failures she was trying to avoid.

As you've seen in this section, cognitive distortions and trauma responses aren't separate. They're two ways of describing the same adaptive mechanisms. Seeing them together gives a fuller picture of how financial self-sabotage takes hold.

Self-Reflection Exercise: Recognizing Self-Sabotage Patterns

A key step in breaking the cycle is to identify how self-sabotage shows up in your financial life. Consider these questions:

What money habits do I keep repeating, even though they cause stress or regret?

What thoughts, emotions, and bodily sensations do I notice before, during, and after taking actions that undermine my financial stability?

Patterns emerge from these reflections. These patterns aren't just unwanted habits. They're signals. Each one tells a deeper story that's asking to be heard.

Bridge to Change

Awareness is powerful, but it's not enough on its own. Healing requires a bridge, one sturdy enough to take you from survival mode into a new way of living. This bridge rests on three supports: safety, self-talk, and intentional action.

At first, the bridge may feel wobbly. Fear urges you to turn back. But each moment you pause, challenge a self-defeating thought, or take a value-aligned action, you add another plank. What once felt fragile grows strong. Here's how to start building that bridge.

Create Safety

For a mind shaped by trauma, self-sabotage often feels like protection. But true safety comes from showing your nervous system that danger has passed and from approaching money with compassion and care.

Calm Your Nervous System

Practice practical strategies that calm your nervous system, allowing you to gradually build a sense of safety around money and prove to your brain that a different, more peaceful financial future is possible. Examples include breathing techniques, gentle physical movement, and pet therapy. Throughout the book are many tools like these: small practices that help your body relearn safety, one moment at a time.

Practice Self-Compassion

Instead of thinking *Why can't I get it together?* try a gentler narrative: *I hit my limit. I handled things with the tools I had. I'm growing, and I get another shot at this.* That simple shift can reshape the way you relate to money. Test this out consistently over a month and notice what happens.

Build Trusted Support

You don't have to do this alone. Sometimes the most powerful thing you can hear is this: *Me too.* That connection can cut through isolation and shame.

Support can look different for everyone: a friend who listens without judgment, a therapist who helps you untangle your story, or a trauma-aware financial coach who helps you set goals and stick with them. Who helps you feel seen? And how might you invite them into your journey to reduce self-sabotage?

Once you feel a foundation of safety, you can start noticing and reshaping the inner dialogue that guides your financial choices.

Shift Your Self-Talk

Self-criticism and low self-worth erode confidence, paving the way for self-sabotage.

Rewrite Your Money Story

If your inner script says, "I'll never get ahead," your actions will often match that belief. Changing your behavior means changing the story beneath it. Think about what you tell yourself when you feel stuck. Are those thoughts true or just familiar? Replace them with something more hopeful and accurate. Over time, those new scripts carve fresh brain pathways (see Chapter 2).

Try this: Rewrite one of your negative money beliefs in a positive light. It could be something like, *I'm learning to manage money better, even if it's slow.*

Journal Your Thoughts

We often don't notice our thoughts until we see them on paper. Journaling connects scattered feelings and reveals patterns. It doesn't need to take a long time. Prompt: When do I tend to sabotage my financial progress? And what emotions and physical sensations show up around those moments?

Reframe Your Beliefs

With your increased clarity, you're ready to reshape the beliefs that trip you up. Question the old patterns and trade them for ones that actually support you. Recognize the part of yourself that tried to protect you: *I appreciate what you were trying to do. And now I'm choosing a new way forward.*

Once your inner dialogue starts to shift, you can pair those thoughts with concrete steps that reinforce new patterns.

Take Intentional Action

Small, steady moves disrupt self-sabotage and point toward growth.

Use Gradual Exposure

Trying to fix everything at once backfires. Start small. If you tend to avoid checking your balance, try reviewing it just once a week with your morning coffee. Focus less on the numbers and more on your courage to look. Celebrate that progress. Momentum builds quietly.

Consider: What's one habit you could shift by just 10%?

Plan Gently

Once you start seeing where things go sideways, you can map a new route. That means creating small, actionable plans you *want* to follow. This approach builds new neural pathways through small, consistent actions that prove safety.

Don't make your plan a punishment. Make it a form of care. If your typical form of self-sabotage is to splurge when feeling unappreciated, what else could meet that need without hurting your finances?

Try this: Use *If-Then* planning. For example, *If I feel that urge to spend after a hard day, then I'll call a friend or take a walk first.*

Reflection Questions

When I get in my own way with money, what am I really trying to protect myself from?

What old money story keeps running in the background of my decisions? And what story do I want to tell instead?

Take Back the Wheel

Self-sabotage doesn't mean you're broken. It means your nervous system is still trying to protect you with old rules. Recognizing that gives you power.

When I realized my money struggles weren't about numbers but about patterns, I was able to disrupt my automatic responses. Pausing before decisions gave me small wins and those wins built on one another.

Change takes time. But every time you steer instead of reacting on autopilot, you prove a different story is possible. You're not stuck in your past. You're capable of building financial peace, one choice at a time.

Key Takeaways

- Self-sabotage is often a survival strategy that grew out of past trauma to serve a protective purpose.
- Trauma can cause changes in thinking that contribute to false money narratives and block progress.
- Healing requires addressing distorted thoughts, emotional patterns, and nervous system responses.
- Awareness marks the trailhead, self-compassion steadies your footing, and small, consistent actions help you move toward change.

When Financial Stress Becomes Too Much to Handle

In this chapter, we've looked at how to interrupt patterns of self-sabotage. But sometimes trauma creates another challenge: Stress hits again and again, for so long that the usual coping tools stop working. What happens when repeated, prolonged stress overwhelms the ability to cope?

For many, the result is complex trauma, a deep wound with lasting effects. In the next chapter, we'll explore how complex trauma shapes our beliefs, bodies, and behaviors.

8

Complex Trauma and Financial Challenges

Money speaks its own language in the context of complex trauma, a language written not in dollars and numbers, but in the ways your mind and body have learned to respond to long-term stress. This disturbance doesn't come from a single wound. It forms over time through prolonged, repeated, often inescapable experiences, most often in relationships.

What may appear on the surface as procrastination, avoidance, or "bad" financial habits hides a deeper story, one of nervous system responses, emotional flashbacks, and an all-around challenging relationship with money.

If you've lived through complex trauma, or even suspect you have, some parts of this chapter may feel heavy. That's normal, and even positive. Recognizing and naming complex trauma creates space for healing. When you view its patterns as survival adaptations, you have the choice to meet your financial life with compassion instead of criticism and respond intentionally rather than automatically.

Move at a pace that feels safe. Healing unfolds in whatever time frame you decide.

What You'll Learn in This Chapter

- How complex trauma differs from single-incident trauma
- How complex trauma shapes money management and decision-making
- Why recovery can feel threatening when parts of you see change as dangerous
- Practical strategies to stay calmer during money tasks
- How patience and the right tools can build financial stability, empowerment, and peace

A Note About This Chapter's Examples

In the sections that follow you'll find a range of experiences with complex trauma. Some readers will recognize themselves in multiple examples, while others may see only glimpses of their own story. Not everyone who's been affected by financial trauma will relate to all the responses shared here. If certain patterns don't match your experience, that doesn't mean your struggles are less valid or that this chapter isn't for you. Trauma happens on a spectrum, and your experience is uniquely yours.

Understanding Complex Trauma: Beyond Single-Incident Trauma

When many people hear the word *trauma*, they picture a *single event*: wartime violence, assault, a natural disaster, or an accident. Complex trauma differs in key ways. While both types of trauma impact daily functioning, including financial behavior, they have key differences:

Single-Incident Trauma	Complex Trauma
Usually stems from a **one-time event**	Develops through **prolonged, repeated experiences**, especially where escape feels impossible
Focus centers on a **specific** traumatic memory	Creates **broad** disruption to identity, regulation, and relationships
Reactions are often tied to **identifiable** triggers	Responses are **diffuse**, shaping core beliefs about the self and the world
Basic trust in self and others may remain intact	**Trust and self-concept** are often deeply damaged

These distinctions aren't absolute, and many symptoms overlap categories. For example, hypervigilance and relationship challenges are common to both types of trauma. The key difference is that complex trauma tends to be more **pervasive** and have a greater impact on the **sense of self**.

Complex financial trauma can develop from:

- Childhood abuse, neglect, abandonment, or lack of safety
- Prolonged financial insecurity or poverty
- Long-term abuse or control by a partner or caregiver
- Predatory lending that creates debt spirals that feel inescapable
- Workplace exploitation, including situations where immigration or documentation status is used for financial control or coercion
- Systemic discrimination or marginalization

In Chapter 3, we saw how childhood experiences shape lifelong financial patterns. Childhood is an especially vulnerable time because of dependency and developing brain structures. But complex trauma can develop at any life stage, whenever someone feels trapped in harmful circumstances they can't escape.

How to Recognize Trauma Patterns in Your Financial Life

You may wonder whether past adversity shapes your relationship with money. Only a qualified professional can diagnose trauma-related conditions, but certain experiences can hint at patterns often seen in people who've lived through prolonged stress:

- You make financial choices impulsively or while feeling disconnected.
- You notice memory gaps around spending or decisions, leaving you surprised or confused later.
- Simple tasks, like checking balances, opening mail, or paying bills, spark numbness, anxiety, panic, or other overwhelming states.
- Setbacks bring waves of hopelessness or shame that feel bigger than the situation itself, and you may keep the details private.
- Your financial patterns create ongoing strain in your relationship with yourself or with others.

These patterns can have many causes, and experiencing them doesn't mean you have a specific condition. If several resonate, the sections ahead will help you explore them through a trauma-aware lens and offer ways to move toward steadier ground.

How Complex Trauma Responses Show Up in Financial Contexts

Complex trauma can surface in many ways around money. The patterns below aren't exhaustive, but they capture common experiences that may feel familiar.

The "Never Quite Safe" Phenomenon

Trigger Pattern: Routine financial decisions, such as checking balances or making purchases, activate hypervigilance. The nervous system reacts as if danger is imminent, even when finances are stable.

Response: The body goes on high alert. You may compulsively check accounts, create excessive backup plans, or struggle to make even small financial choices without exhaustive research. Complex trauma often leaves you feeling hopeless about ever being truly safe. This is unlike single-incident trauma, where the path to restoring safety, though difficult, can feel clearer.

Impact: This constant vigilance drains enormous energy. Everyday financial tasks create decision fatigue and emotional exhaustion.

Financial Consequences: Money sits in multiple "just in case" accounts rather than being invested. Career opportunities involving risk get declined. Time that could support financial growth is consumed by checking and rechecking details.

Helen's Story

"I check my accounts at least six times a day. I know it's overkill. I have more than enough in savings. But it doesn't feel safe unless I see the numbers. Again and again.

"My partner says I'm obsessed. Maybe I am. But when I try to stop, I panic. My mind races with every worst-case scenario: job loss, recession, medical emergency. So I track every penny. I plan for every disaster.

"The irony? I don't have the energy to apply for promotions or grow my income. All that planning to stay safe keeps me stuck."

Emotional Echoes in Financial Situations

Trigger Pattern: Financial situations that echo past trauma can set off emotional flashbacks. For example, receiving unexpected bills, needing to ask for money, or facing financial negotiations, even in safe circumstances, may trigger you.

Response: The same emotional intensity of the original trauma floods back. Entire emotional states re-emerge more than specific memories. Rationally you may know you're safe, but your nervous system and emotions react as if you're back in danger.

Impact: You delay important financial decisions or make them from an emotional flashback state rather than present reality. Your choices prioritize short-term relief over long-term well-being.

Financial Consequences: Salary negotiations fall short of market value. Opportunities are filtered through the lens of past trauma rather than present possibilities. Decisions can stir identity confusion or internal conflict.

Riley's Story

When Riley's colleague suggested she apply for a promotion, her heart raced and flashbacks surged. As a child, asking her parents for anything brought emotional abuse.

Don't push it. Just be grateful, whispered her old childhood voice.

Rationally, Riley knew she deserved the role. But in that moment, she felt small, scared, and powerless, like the girl who had learned that asking for things came at a price.

No, I'm happy where I am, she heard herself tell her co-worker, even though Riley would have welcomed the higher-paid position. Later, she wondered why once again she felt frozen in place.

Complex trauma responses manifest differently for different people. Let's look at another common pattern.

Relational Challenges

Trauma creates many kinds of relationship hurdles, as we'll explore in Chapter 10. Here, we focus on boundary-setting because it is so deeply connected with complex trauma.

Trigger Pattern: If past attempts at setting boundaries brought you abandonment, punishment, or danger, saying no can feel threatening. So when family members or people close to you ask you for money, your trauma responses get activated.

Response: Setting any boundaries at all may be difficult. The boundaries you're able to set may swing wildly, like overgiving for years then cutting people off. These inconsistencies reflect survival responses like fawning (giving money to stay connected) or freezing (becoming immobilized when conflicting needs collide). Even when you maintain boundaries, intense guilt often follows (see Chapter 11 on survivor's guilt).

Impact: Boundary inconsistency creates chaos in both finances and relationships. Your good money practices collapse under pressure, while your trust in relationships erodes.

Financial Consequences: Emergency funds drain. Retirement savings get compromised. Financial plans are derailed by repeated requests for loans.

Vin's Story

Vin barely escaped bankruptcy after co-signing a loan a family member defaulted on. He swore he'd never mix money and family again. But when his sister cried about needing money for rent, his trauma response overrode that rule. Memories of childhood abandonment surged. On some level, he feared that saying no meant losing her. He emptied his emergency fund, then spent weeks swinging between panic attacks and numbness.

Complex trauma responses like Vin's often trace back to childhood. These stem from the relational foundation of the trauma itself, for example, abandonment or the repeated violation of a child's physical or emotional limits by the very caregivers they depended on for survival and safety. Relationships are learned to be simultaneously vital and dangerous, leading to a damaged sense of self, pervasive mistrust, and difficulty setting healthy boundaries in adulthood.[47]

The Interplay of the Inner Critic, Shame, and Self-Worth

Trigger Pattern: Financial decisions, mistakes, or challenges often awaken the inner critic, a harsh voice amplified by complex trauma. The critic frames even minor setbacks as failures and fuels shame.

Response: The critic attacks your self-worth, using everyday financial glitches as evidence of your inadequacy while dismissing your successes. These attacks promote a sense of worthlessness and may lead you to hide struggles, disregard solutions, or self-sabotage in ways that confirm the critic's predictions.

Impact: This toxic loop makes rational financial action difficult. Each response reinforces the belief that you're defective.

Financial Consequences: When the inner critic drives decisions, outcomes vary but often carry genuine costs. Assistance programs go unused. Investment opportunities are avoided. Financial education feels threatening. Debt grows from avoidance and penalties.

Aisha's Story

Although Aisha ran her own successful consulting business, her inner critic told her she was "terrible with money" and "undeserving of success." When she needed to raise her rates, it called her "greedy" and "a fraud." Losing a client became proof she was a "failure." These attacks, rooted in a past financially abusive relationship, eroded Aisha's confidence, decision-making ability, and joy in her achievements.

Disconnecting When Handling Financial Tasks

Trigger Pattern: Financial tasks can trigger dissociation, an involuntary coping mechanism that disconnects you from your thoughts, feelings, or surroundings. You may find yourself "checking out" when doing things like paying bills, budgeting, or banking. Dissociation exists on a spectrum. Everyone occasionally spaces out or goes on autopilot. That's normal. What distinguishes trauma-related dissociation is that it's involuntary, happens frequently during specific triggers like financial tasks, and interferes with your ability to perform these tasks effectively.

Response: You may feel as if being in a dream, in a fog, on autopilot, or outside your body. Sometimes you may forget financial decisions or make purchases you don't recall. These moments of disconnection happen without your choosing them.

Impact: Awareness slips, and planning becomes difficult.

Financial Consequences: Late fees pile up, deadlines get missed, credit scores drop, and funds vanish without a clear record.

Jamie's Story

Jamie earns well but racks up late fees. Sitting with her bills, she stares for hours, unaware of time. Sometimes, purchases appear on her card she doesn't remember making. The bills don't scare her as much as the blank spaces in her memory. Each forgotten charge feels like proof that part of her is still living in survival mode, even in safety.

Jamie's dissociation is common in complex trauma. Her repeated overwhelm has trained her nervous system to "check out."

If these stories feel heavy, that's understandable. Remember: Recognizing these patterns is the first step toward changing them. And change is possible.

The stories show just how layered the effects of complex trauma can be, intertwining personal history, survival responses, emotions, and identity. To navigate these layers, it helps to know how trauma shapes the nervous system, especially in financial contexts, and what you can do about it. That's where the concept of the *window of tolerance* comes in.

The Window of Tolerance: A Framework for Understanding Financial Functioning

The *window of tolerance*, introduced by Dr. Dan Siegel,[48] describes the zone where you can think clearly, process emotions, and make sound decisions. Inside this window, financial tasks feel manageable. Step outside it, and the nervous system flips into survival mode, a response that once kept you safe but that now can erode stability.

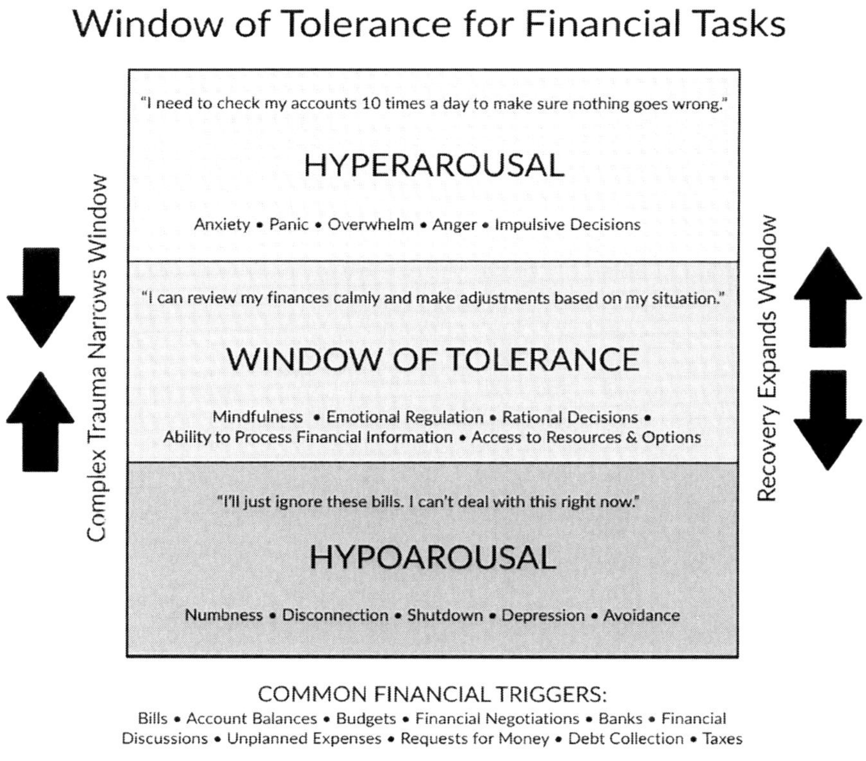

How Complex Trauma Narrows the Financial Window

Complex trauma shrinks your capacity to stay regulated during money tasks. Everyday money events, like an unexpected bill or a partner asking about expenses, can suddenly narrow the window of tolerance. What feels routine for others becomes an emotional minefield to someone with a history of trauma.

After long-term exposure to stressors, the cumulative damage fundamentally alters a person's perception of self, others, and the future, making it harder to return to a baseline of safety and stability.

The nervous system may swing from *hyperarousal* (panic, obsessive checking) to *hypoarousal* (numbness, shutdown) within minutes. Consistent financial management becomes almost impossible unless you have strategies to gently bring yourself back inside the window.

To widen this window for financial tasks, healing must address trauma and money together.

The Unique Challenge of Financial Recovery for People Living with Complex Trauma

The long-term, repeated nature of the events leading to complex trauma creates more entrenched brain pathways and survival strategies.

Trying to fix finances without addressing trauma is like patching a leaky boat while ignoring the storm. You need both inner healing and practical money strategies. Without both, progress slips away.

Making these changes is challenging. Complex trauma reshapes identity. Parts of the self that learned to survive may resist change, seeing it as dangerous. They whisper: *You'll just fail again.* Or *Money isn't safe.*

That resistance often shows up as defiance, sabotage, or overwhelm, especially when you face tasks like examining past financial behaviors or creating new money habits.

But remember: The parts of you that developed these financial patterns weren't trying to ruin your future. They were trying to save your life. Honoring this wisdom while gently updating their strategies is your path forward.

Max's Experience

When Max's therapist suggested creating a budget, younger traumatized parts of him flooded with fear. Budgeting reminded him of times when having needs led to abuse. He could handle about five minutes with his finances before becoming either so anxious he couldn't sit still or so mentally foggy he couldn't process the numbers.

Switching away from the idea of a traditional budget, his therapist broke tasks into small, tolerable pieces. She and Max experimented with combinations of income review and grounding practices that reminded Max he was safe now. He especially liked the 5-5-5 ritual: five minutes of grounding, five minutes on a money task, and five minutes on self-care. Over months, he slowly expanded his window, eventually handling fifteen-minute sessions on a money task without distress. What once felt unbearable became sustainable.

Small practices help you stay within your window of tolerance during money tasks. But building long-term financial stability with complex trauma requires additional support structures that work with your nervous system.

The following approaches create sustainable pathways for financial healing. You don't need to implement all of them at once. Choose what resonates and build from there.

Creating Financial Safety Nets that Support the Nervous System

Think of this as building guardrails, not cages. The goal isn't to control yourself but to protect your essentials when trauma responses cloud your thinking.

Practical safeguards might include:

- A system that's as automated as possible (automated deposits, transfers, and bill payments)
- A financial crisis plan with clear, simple steps you (or a trusted person) can follow when money feels overwhelming
- Visual cues or calendar prompts that interrupt dissociation or detachment by keeping you focused on key tasks
- A short weekly money check-in: five minutes at the same time each week to deal with any new or unexpected tasks
- A pairing of financial duties with safety cues: whatever combination of soothing approaches works for you
- A division of more complex tasks into trauma-manageable segments so you never face everything at once

These supports work *with* your nervous system, not against it. They give you a baseline of safety to rely on.

Working with Trauma-Informed Professionals

Sometimes a powerful move is to invite support.

If this feels right for you, look for professionals who adapt to your needs, avoid shaming, and prioritize psychological safety alongside financial progress. They can help you by:

- Offering compassionate accountability without blame
- Supporting both the personal and practical sides of money healing
- Teaching in ways that feel accessible, especially in hard seasons

You might feel some resistance to this kind of support; that's part of the process. Resistance serves as an armor: a natural, instinctual, logical response to avoid re-experiencing traumatic memories. If you decide to engage in recovery work with others, it's important to prioritize trust and safety and go at your own pace.

Integrating Somatic Practices into Recovery Work

Somatic practices, approaches that work with the body's response to trauma, can powerfully reshape your relationship with money. Trauma lingers in the body, and recovery must involve the body too. As Bessel van der Kolk describes in *The Body Keeps the Score*, unresolved trauma is stored and triggered physically.[49]

Practical ways to bring the body into money work:

- Practicing deep breathing while checking accounts
- Scanning the body to notice where tension shows up during money discussions

- Taking movement breaks to release stored stress
- Using "resourcing" when overwhelmed: recalling a safe memory, holding a grounding object, or drawing on physical sensations of comfort and strength

If you remember one thing: Your body can guide you back to safety, even with money.

Using *Parts Work* to Soothe Trauma Responses

Complex trauma often leads to a fragmented sense of self,[50] and *parts work* offers a non-pathologizing framework to heal this fragmentation by bringing these voices into dialogue and balance.

For many living with complex trauma, different parts of the self have conflicting relationships with money. One part may say *We need to look at the credit card bill*, and another part may answer, *We'll be punished if we do.* Parts work helps by:

- Identifying "financial protector parts" that avoid or control money tasks
- Connecting with vulnerable "exile parts" that carry fear or shame about money
- Building dialogue between the adult self and younger parts around safety and the need for change

This work softens the inner conflict and helps all parts move toward financial healing.

At this point, you can see that financial recovery goes far beyond numbers. It involves nervous system regulation, body awareness, and inner dialogue.

These tools aren't quick fixes, but they create footholds. They're offered as ideas for exploration, but you're the expert on your own life and you're the one in charge.

Moving Forward with Hope and Resilience

Living with complex trauma responses while trying to manage money can feel like climbing a steep hill in heavy boots. But now you have those footholds. Once you see how trauma shapes money behaviors, you can reduce the weight of old survival patterns and begin making choices that reflect your present needs and values. What does this journey actually look like? Here's one person's experience.

Damien's Story

Five years ago, Damien couldn't open a bill without spiraling into panic. Growing up with a volatile parent who exploded over money left him wired to expect danger in every financial task.

Today, after seeing a financial therapist, Damien has built systems that work with his nervous system. He grounds himself with somatic techniques before checking accounts, breaks tasks into tolerable segments, and leans on a support system that offers accountability without shame.

Triggers still show up, but his window of tolerance has widened. Most importantly, Damien now meets his financial responses with compassion instead of criticism. He recognizes those patterns once protected him in chaos. That shift from judgment to understanding has been as healing as any practical tool.

Healing takes time, and it's okay to start small. Maybe you approach one financial habit differently. Maybe you search for a supportive coach or therapist. Maybe you experiment with mindfulness during money decisions. Progress doesn't mean avoiding setbacks. It means daring to try something different, one choice at a time. Bit by bit, those choices add up to another kind of safety: one grounded in agency and resilience, not just survival.

Reflection Questions

How has understanding the connection between complex trauma and financial behavior reshaped your view of your own money patterns or those of others?

What strategies help you stay grounded when financial tasks feel triggering?

Which of your personal strengths could you lean on as you navigate the challenges at the intersection of trauma and money?

Key Takeaways

- Complex financial trauma affects core identity, making even routine tasks feel overwhelming.
- It often shows up through emotional echoes, relational challenges, attacks by the inner critic, a sense of never quite being safe, and other patterns.
- The Window of Tolerance describes a zone where you can think clearly, process emotions, and make sound decisions.
- The Window of Tolerance and other approaches make it possible to achieve financial wellness even with complex trauma.

Healing happens when you honor both financial and emotional needs, moving at a pace that feels safe. Some days bring progress, others setbacks. That rhythm doesn't mean failure. It's the nature of healing.

Easing trauma symptoms means clearing away the obstacles we place in our own path. But there's another layer to this story, one that's often overlooked: Our mental health doesn't sit on the sidelines while we untangle our financial lives. It actively shapes how we experience money, and money, in turn, profoundly influences our mental health.

This two-way relationship can either trap us in destructive cycles or, when understood, become a path toward well-being. That's where we're headed in our next chapter.

9

Money and Mental Health: Breaking the Spiral

Financial adversity is challenging for anyone, but it's especially hard to navigate when paired with mental health struggles. In a recent survey, 43% of Americans reported money affects their mental health negatively.[51]

Money and mental health don't run parallel. They form a tightly intertwined system. Existing mental health conditions can make someone more vulnerable to financial difficulties, and financial difficulties, in turn, can trigger or worsen mental health challenges.[52]

To make sense of this connection, we'll unpack the two-way relationship between financial instability and mental health and explore strategies to disrupt the cycle.

What You'll Learn in This Chapter

- How existing mental health conditions can contribute to money problems
- How money problems, in turn, can trigger or intensify mental health challenges, creating a self-reinforcing cycle
- How chronic financial stress can embed itself as financial trauma, affecting well-being beyond mere discomfort or everyday money worries
- Why traditional financial advice often falls short for those navigating the complex interplay of mental health and money wounds, and how a trauma-informed lens offers a more helpful path
- Why addressing financial or mental health issues in isolation is rarely enough, and how a whole-person approach supports true healing and progress

Before we dive into these dynamics, it's important to understand where this chapter fits in a larger story about how financial trauma moves beyond the individual.

The Relational Web of Financial Trauma

Financial trauma rarely stays contained within the person experiencing it. More often, it impacts that person's loved ones and close contacts. While the previous chapters have explored how trauma shapes our individual psychology and behaviors, the next three chapters examine a crucial truth: Our money wounds affect everyone we're connected to, and theirs affect us.

These chapters form a connected exploration of how financial trauma moves through our relationships:

In this chapter (Chapter 9), we'll explore the two-way relationship between money and mental health. This creates ripple effects that touch our closest relationships, often through isolation, conflict, or the strain of watching someone we love struggle.

In Chapter 10, we'll zoom in on romantic partnerships specifically: the unique challenges that arise when people with their own money wounds try to build a shared financial life. Here, financial trauma becomes interpersonal in a most intimate way: in how couples communicate, make decisions, handle power dynamics, and navigate trust.

In Chapter 11, we'll shift to examine a different relational dimension: the guilt that can arise when you've achieved financial stability while family or community members continue to struggle. This survivor's guilt creates its own relational patterns, ones that can sabotage progress and strain the very connections you're trying to honor.

Together, these three chapters reveal that healing from financial trauma isn't just an individual journey. It's also a relational one. The patterns we carry affect how we connect with partners, family, and community. And those relationships, in turn, shape our capacity to heal.

Understanding these dynamics doesn't just help us navigate our own recovery. It helps us extend compassion to those around us who may be struggling with their own unseen money wounds.

Let's begin by exploring the powerful connection between mental health and money, and why addressing one without the other so rarely leads to lasting change.

The Trauma Lens on Mental Health and Money

Trauma adds a crucial layer to the relationship between mental health and personal finance. Pre-existing mental health challenges can increase vulnerability to financial trauma. Depression, for example, can impair decision-making, leading to financial circumstances ripe for trauma. Anxiety can drive hypervigilance over money, a state which can feel supportive in the short term but gradually makes money a source of ongoing stress and harm.

When these financial pressures overwhelm our capacity to cope and threaten our sense of safety, we experience chronic stress. Over time, our nervous system responds protectively. This can show up as preoccupation over financial threats, avoidance of money matters, or intrusive thoughts about financial disaster. These trauma responses can mimic, intensify, or even trigger mental health conditions.

It's important to recognize that trauma responses operate in a different way than everyday stress or many common mental health challenges. The chronic activation of our stress response systems can alter brain structure and function, particularly in areas governing threat detection, emotional regulation, and decision-making, as explored in Chapter 2. Financial trauma reshapes a person's fundamental sense of safety in the world and alters their identity and relationship with money in profound ways.

What began as financial difficulty paired with mental health challenges can evolve into financial trauma, a fundamental rewiring of how our nervous system responds to money. This transformation is what makes the cycle so difficult to break: We're now dealing with a traumatized nervous system treating financial situations as existential threats.

How Mental Health Affects Personal Finances

Symptoms associated with mental illnesses can make managing money harder, increasing vulnerability to financial crises. For example:

- **Impulsivity and impaired decision-making**, associated with bipolar and some other disorders, can lead to unsound choices, like gambling or taking on unmanageable debt.
- **Avoidance behaviors**, common in anxiety and depression, can cause delinquent payments, damaged credit, and missed opportunities to fix problems early.
- **Difficulty maintaining steady employment**, a consequence of many serious mental illnesses, can create income instability that compounds over time.
- **The stigma and isolation of living with a mental disorder** can reduce access to guidance and support during periods of financial strain.

How Financial Difficulties Affect Mental Health

Financial adversity can profoundly affect mental health. For instance:

- **Chronic financial instability**—whether resulting from a large-scale economic crisis like a recession or long-term personal hardship—is associated with higher rates of anxiety, depression, sleep disturbances, low self-esteem and self-confidence, substance use disorders, and suicidal thoughts and actions.[53] Poverty is a key adverse childhood experience (ACE), raising the risk of mental health problems in adulthood, as explored in Chapter 5.
- **Sudden financial shocks** can lead to intense emotions like hopelessness, overwhelm, and a loss of control, as well as mental health conditions such as chronic stress, anxiety, and depression.

- **Couples' money issues** are a significant source of stress and can lead to depression, anxiety, and instability in the relationship. One partner's financial strain can directly impact the mental well-being of the other.
- **Family financial strain** can erode parents' ability to create a supportive environment for their children. Kids in financially strained homes often experience similar mental health challenges as their parents (stress, anxiety, depression) along with behavioral and academic issues and higher exposure to negative peer influences.[54]
- **Expenses related to mental health treatment** for serious psychiatric conditions and addiction, such as hospitalization, residential care, legal fees, or lost wages, can create financial and emotional hardship for an individual and their family; this hardship can complicate long-term recovery.
- **High-stress debt** can fuel depression, anxiety, and suicidal ideation, especially when payments feel unmanageable or shame enters the picture.[55]

Understanding how mental health affects finances, and vice versa, is essential. The true complexity emerges when these forces interact, amplifying each other in a self-reinforcing cycle.

The Interaction: A Vicious Cycle

Mental health challenges and financial stress are more than parallel struggles. They're deeply intertwined forces that amplify each other in ways that can feel relentless and unpredictable.

Take Eva, who lives with **social anxiety**. She avoids job interviews, networking, and salary negotiations, so she earns less than peers with similar qualifications. The resulting financial strain and shame feed her withdrawal, making it even harder to recover emotionally or financially.

Or consider Theo, who has **bipolar disorder**. During manic episodes, he takes significant financial risks: overspending, building up credit card debt, gambling, and investing recklessly. When the mania ends, the fallout brings shame and regret, deepening his depression and destabilizing his mood. Recovery from both his financial and mental health crises becomes more complex.

Then there's Neve, whose **substance use** drains her resources and leaves her without savings. Her vulnerability to unexpected expenses produces fear and pressure and makes it harder for her to escape both poverty and addiction.

These interconnected patterns show how mental health and financial challenges weave together, each reinforcing the other.

Understanding the Patterns Through Stories: The Mind-Money Connection in Action

It's crucial to acknowledge both parts of the cycle. Treating mental illness while ignoring financial realities or fixing financial struggles while overlooking emotional tolls leaves people feeling stuck. True progress requires a whole-person approach.

To see how this principle unfolds in real life, let's use a trauma lens to look at the case studies of two individuals: Quinn, whose depression quietly eroded her financial stability, and Kai, a high achiever whose anxiety tangled with cultural pressures and financial risk. Together, these stories illustrate both the shutdown response (Quinn) and the hypervigilance response (Kai) that can emerge when mental health and money collide.

The Depression Cascade: A Case Study

Quinn, a video editor, had long managed her moderate depression. She built systems that kept her financially stable even during low-energy periods: a simple budget and automatic payments for rent, her car loan, and utilities.

The First Shifts

After a loss in the family, Quinn's depression deepened. Though she kept her job, her declining mental health gradually affected her executive function, the brain's "air traffic control" system for daily tasks.

At first, the changes were subtle. She shuffled unopened bills from table to counter to coffee table. Email alerts got marked as "read" without opening. She'd start to log into her bank account, then close the browser: *I'll deal with this after dinner,* she told herself. But dinner came and went.

As the pile of bills grew, Quinn's responses shifted beyond ordinary stress. Each time she noticed the mail, her body shut down. Her mind went blank, her limbs felt heavy, and she found herself without any sense of what to do next. It was as if her system had hit an invisible wall: a shutdown that left her feeling disconnected from her own ability to act.

She began rerouting through the kitchen to avoid the stack of envelopes. When her phone chimed with reminders, she dismissed them unread, her chest tightening. The sound of the mail truck brought dread.

The Financial Impact

Over months, unpaid bills piled up, not because she lacked money but because she ignored the reminders. Late fees stacked. A subscription payment she meant to cancel overdrew an account she'd forgotten to fund.

The hardest blow came when her credit score dropped by 55 points. Higher interest rates on her credit card intensified her stress and shame.

The Mental Health Spiral

Each financial setback deepened Quinn's negative self-image and depression. She berated herself for failing at "simple" tasks and replayed old scripts about being "lousy with money."

With each new problem, her fear of opening mail or checking accounts grew stronger, cementing a sense of helplessness.

The Reinforcing Bond

The mental health–money cycle took on a life of its own. Quinn's depression made money management harder, while the financial fallout worsened her depression. As both sets of problems deepened, recovery seemed further and further out of reach.

Impact on Daily Life

The strain bled into every part of her life. Chronic stress disrupted her sleep and digestion. To catch up on bills, she worked extra hours, leading to burnout. To hide her struggles, she avoided friends and financial conversations. Blaming herself, she came to believe she was unworthy of help.

Through the Trauma Lens

Quinn's story shows how mental health struggles and financial stress can escalate into financial trauma. Her shift from mild avoidance to full shutdown was more than depression. It was her nervous system escalating its response to overwhelming financial stress.

Each financial setback reinforced her belief that money matters were dangerous, triggering a freeze response when she faced these tasks. As we explored in Chapter 2, this is the hallmark of financial trauma: The brain and body treat money situations as a threat, shutting down rational decision-making.

If the cycle had been interrupted, Quinn's trajectory could have been different. (We'll return to this in the "Out of the Spiral" section later in the chapter.)

While Quinn's story shines a light on depression, the next case study reveals how anxiety can pull even high achievers into destructive cycles.

The Achievement Pressure Spiral

Kai, a successful startup founder, lived with high-functioning anxiety that had always run in the background of his achievements. For years, he managed it. But when external stressors threatened both his business and his sense of identity, the balance collapsed.

The First Cracks in Success

An economic downturn shook Kai's startup. As revenue fell, he dreaded laying off valued employees or disappointing investors. What might have been ordinary business problems became threats to his very identity, magnified by cultural messages equating success with worth.

The Mental Health Impact: Anxiety Behind the Mask

The stress pushed Kai's anxiety into overdrive. A relentless inner critic plagued him with intrusive thoughts: *You're not smart enough for this,* the voice would tell him during board meetings. *You've just been lucky until now.* These thoughts of inadequacy and fraudulence made the shame of failure feel more dangerous than any financial loss.

He worked harder, micromanaged obsessively, and told himself it was discipline, when it was really anxious hypervigilance. Panic attacks struck before investor meetings. Sleepless nights stretched into hours of "what if" thinking. Cultural stigma around failure only sharpened these responses, making every setback feel catastrophic.

Buying Stability at Any Cost

Anxiety-driven shame kept Kai silent. Instead of reaching out to advisors or peers, he convinced himself that asking for help would expose his incompetence. So, he shouldered the burden alone.

He extended risky credit terms, took on high-interest bridge loans, and restructured deals without legal review. To avoid layoffs, he drained his savings and took on personal debt. Though he cared for his team, the deeper driver was fear of being seen as unsuccessful.

The Vicious Feedback Loop

Financial pressure fueled Kai's anxiety, and anxiety drove reckless financial decisions that created more pressure. Each misstep confirmed his belief that he was a fraud. The very achievement orientation that once powered his success now trapped him.

The Hidden Cost of Success

Kai's health faltered under stress and insomnia. Relationships grew tense as his anxious preoccupation consumed him. Unable to untangle his self-worth from his company's fate, he lived under constant siege. Outwardly successful, he was inwardly unraveling.

Through the Trauma Lens

Kai's story shows how anxiety can ripen into financial trauma when professional identity becomes the bedrock of personal safety. His intrusive thoughts weren't just a symptom of anxiety. They reflected a nervous system treating financial challenges as existential threats.

Cultural pressures around success intensified the cycle, but the engine was trauma: hypervigilance as obsessive monitoring, panic before high-stakes meetings, secrecy and isolation driven by shame. These weren't just poor choices. They were trauma responses that blocked him from reaching out for the help he needed.

Quinn's and Kai's stories show us two different faces of the same fundamental dynamic: When mental health struggles and financial stress intertwine, they create self-reinforcing cycles that can feel inescapable. Quinn's nervous system responded with shutdown and freeze, Kai's with hypervigilance and compulsive action. Yet both were trapped in patterns where each setback confirmed their deepest fears and drove behaviors that created more setbacks.

But here's what matters most: These cycles, however entrenched, are not permanent. Breaking free is possible, and it often begins more simply than we might imagine.

Out of the Spiral

Breaking free from the spiral begins with awareness. The first shift comes when we notice how financial triggers and their responses feed each other, keeping us caught in a loop that feels impossible to escape.

Healing for Quinn and Kai began with noticing their patterns and deepened with small steps toward change. Awareness plus action broke the cycle, and the same is possible for you.

Often change begins with a quiet act of defiance. Imagine Quinn choosing to open just one bill and pay it. That single act, however small, sparks relief. A week later, she opens another. Slowly, avoidance loosens its hold. Was it easy? Not at all. But gradually she regains a sense of control.

Now picture her channeling that momentum into saving $5 a day, or meeting with a money coach, or taking a financial course. Small, consistent actions don't just improve finances. They ripple into confidence, relationships, and health.

For Kai, the turning point came when he finally confided in a mentor about the pressure he was under. That conversation didn't solve his financial problems, but it pierced his isolation and challenged the belief that asking for help meant admitting failure.

He started small: delegating one decision he'd been micromanaging, then another. Each act of letting go felt uncomfortable, even risky, but it also brought unexpected relief.

Breaking negative cycles doesn't mean achieving perfection. It means finding the courage to move once, then again, trusting that small shifts can compound into profound change.

Integration: Understanding the Patterns

Across these stories, one theme stands out: The cycles of mental health and financial struggles don't just persist. They gain momentum.

A missed bill leads to shame, which fuels avoidance, which triggers late fees and more shame. Anxiety over performance drives impulsive decisions, which confirm self-doubt, which sharpens the anxiety. Step by step, the spiral tightens.

These loops seldom develop overnight. They compound gradually beneath the surface until the damage is too big to ignore. By the time the full weight is felt, the cycle already feels overwhelming.

Traditional financial advice often fails in these moments because it focuses on symptoms rather than root causes. Telling someone with depression to "track every dollar" or urging someone with anxiety to "just stop overspending" ignores the deeper psychological and nervous system forces driving behaviors. Without addressing these underlying realities, advice can feel more than unhelpful. It can feel invalidating.

Breaking these cycles takes more than willpower or quick fixes. It requires self-awareness to name the pattern, courage to disrupt it, and deliberate action to change course. That may sound like a lot, and it is. But it can begin with manageable shifts that build momentum over time.

The cruel irony is that the very resources we need, like therapy, coaching, or financial breathing room, often feel out of reach because of the spiral itself. Cost barriers, lack of time, or limited energy can reinforce the loop.

That's why the first step isn't perfection. It's acknowledgment. Naming the cycle shifts the ground. And recognizing that these cycles are not personal failings can loosen the grip of shame and open space for change.

From Awareness to Action

Try This: A Small Shift Toward Change

You don't have to overhaul your finances or fix everything at once. But if you're feeling stuck, one small, intentional action can help shift your energy and signal to your nervous system that change is possible.

Pick one of these, or create your own:

- Check one account and notice your emotional response without judgment.
- Set a five-minute timer and jot down what financial safety means to you.
- Share one financial fear with a trusted friend, coach, or journal.
- Choose one value-driven financial action you could take this week, however minor.

You're not trying to solve everything. You're simply proving to yourself that disruption is possible. That's enough for today.

Disruption is often the crucial first step; it proves change can happen. But for sustained healing, especially when trauma responses are deeply embedded, additional support is needed.

A Trauma-Aware Approach to Recovery

Effective recovery can take many forms.

No one else knows your experiences, values, or pain the way you do. Trust that wisdom. It will guide you toward the right place to begin your recovery. Here are some ideas:

- **Trauma-informed financial therapy**. This integrates money and mental health. It might look like working with a therapist who understands that avoidance of bank statements isn't laziness but a nervous system response.
- **Somatic (body-based) practices**. These regulate the nervous system's response to financial triggers. For example, you might do a body scan or a breathwork practice before viewing an account.
- **Financial self-care routines**. These rebuild safety and agency around money. Intentionally examining your finances at regular intervals fosters knowledge, control, and confidence.
- **Self-compassion work**. This counters the shame tied to financial trauma. You might try journaling as if writing to a dear friend in your situation.

Throughout this chapter, we've seen several pathways to healing: Quinn's story shows how small actions can rebuild momentum, while Kai's situation highlights the importance of separating identity from financial outcomes and seeking support.

Whether you relate more to Quinn's avoidance or Kai's over-control, the opening begins in the same place: noticing the pattern and making one tiny, courageous movement forward. From there hope and healing expand.

Wherever you are on your journey, remember this: Transformation is possible, and you don't have to do it alone.

Reflection Questions

Think back to a time when money stress weighed on your mind (even if this didn't result in a diagnosis), or when a mental health challenge made handling finances harder. What emotions or bodily reactions did you notice? How did money and mental health seem to feed off each other?

What's a micro action you could take this week to start disrupting a negative cycle, something that signals to yourself that change is possible?

Key Takeaways

- Financial and mental health challenges fuel each other in self-reinforcing spirals.
- Without disruption, these spirals don't just persist; they gain momentum.
- Ongoing financial stress combined with mental health challenges creates fertile ground for financial trauma.
- Recognizing trauma responses is essential for effective intervention.
- Breaking free begins with awareness and micro steps that prove change is possible.

Financial trauma can feel deeply isolating, but we rarely face money challenges alone. In intimate relationships, our financial wounds don't just resurface. They collide with our partner's, creating dynamics that can feel confusing and painful. The next chapter explores how past money trauma shapes present-day partnerships, and how couples can transform financial conflict into opportunities for healing and deeper connection.

10

Financial Trauma in Relationships: The Hidden Cost

When people form relationships, they bring more than their assets and debts. They bring money stories and, sometimes, trauma responses. Challenges that once seemed manageable alone can intensify once two partners share expenses, plan together, or depend on each other for financial security.

For those carrying financial trauma, money becomes a silent third person in the relationship, shaping trust, intimacy, power, and stability.

What might look like a simple disagreement about spending can actually be two trauma responses colliding: one partner's hypervigilance meeting the other's avoidance, both rooted in old wounds.

The good news? With awareness and communication, couples can turn financial challenges into opportunities for deeper connection and growth.

What You'll Learn in This Chapter

- How past financial trauma resurfaces in relationships through conflict, power struggles, secrecy, and withdrawal
- Common issues in financially intimate relationships and how to recognize them as trauma responses, not personal shortcomings
- How inherited money beliefs from childhood shape the way partners relate to finances
- How dynamics like unequal contributions or unrealistic expectations reinforce emotional wounds
- Practical ways partners can navigate financial trauma together with greater awareness, safety, and connection

How Financial Wounds Resurface

Financial trauma echoes through both the practical and emotional layers of a partnership. Left unrecognized, these money wounds quietly distort how couples talk, plan, and place trust in each other.

Financial trauma often reappears in how partners pool resources, set goals, or make joint decisions. Tasks like these can reopen old wounds and spark cycles of tension, control, or secrecy.

Conflict and Tension

We wear our childhood and adult money stories like invisible backpacks. Financial disagreements often unzip them and expose the pain and the protective mechanisms that we carry.

What starts as a simple disagreement about spending can quickly become charged with fear, vulnerability, and unresolved pain. Even a routine purchase can trigger memories of scarcity or instability, igniting emotional exchanges that expose each partner's complex history with money.

Here's how these trauma responses over money can show up specifically in relationships:

- Fight – Criticizing, blaming, or policing spending
- Flight – Avoiding money talks or ignoring bills
- Freeze – Feeling paralyzed and unable to participate in financial matters
- Fawn – Agreeing to joint financial arrangements that feel unwise or unsafe

What makes these reactions tricky is that they happen unconsciously. They come from the limbic system (the brain's emotional engine) rather than the prefrontal cortex (our rational regulator), as explored in Chapter 2.

These reactions rarely stay confined to the argument itself. Over time, they can subtly reshape the balance of power in the relationship.

Power Dynamics

Money can become a silent weapon in relationships. One partner's wallet can act like a dimmer switch, slowly lowering the other's sense of independence. These dynamics reach beyond bills or budgets. They extend to autonomy, identity, and whose voice carries more weight.

Even when couples enjoy a healthy relationship and similar income, a financial power imbalance can emerge, as it did for Noah and Jen.

Throughout Noah's childhood, his parents fought loudly and bitterly about money. The chaos made him feel unsafe. Now, even though he and Jen share equal influence in most areas of their life, Noah surrenders all financial control to her. He may silently disagree with some of her choices, but his avoidance shields him from the distress that echoes his past. The trade-off? Safety at the expense of agency. The path forward, explored later in this chapter, lies in recognizing these old patterns and developing new ways to talk about money that feel secure for both partners.

Whether caused by chronic trauma, devastating loss, or past financial abuse, money wounds can make normal interdependence feel threatening. Responses range from rigid control to defensive pushback to total abdication. Ironically, these strategies often backfire, creating more stress and reinforcing the very pain they're meant to ease.

Spending decisions carry symbolic weight, reshaping the emotional balance between partners. And sometimes the most damaging power dynamics come not from control, but from concealment.

Hidden Financial Issues

What stays unspoken can carry as much emotional weight as what's shared.

Money secrets act like buried fault lines waiting to shake the relationship. They often spring from shame or fear, rooted in past moments of financial vulnerability.

Hiding money details isn't just about numbers. It's about protection. These choices reflect the brain's effort to shield us from judgment, rejection, or pain, even when that protection undermines trust.

As we saw in Chapter 6, secrecy can serve as a shelter from shame for a time, but it also corrodes intimacy. Once money secrets take root, they don't just strain the budget. They change how partners connect and feel safe with each other.

Emotional Impact

Financial trauma seeps into relationships in subtle but profound ways. It can transform what should be a refuge into a minefield. Every conversation about money carries the risk of stepping on something explosive like an old worry or a buried frustration. Each challenge becomes a trigger, reawakening stories about safety, worth, and survival.

The pressure of that stress can erode closeness, creating distance that extends far beyond money itself.

While the emotional toll is immediate, the roots run deeper. Our triggers rarely start with us; they often begin generations back.

Generational Patterns

We learn money like we learn language: through our families. As discussed in Chapter 3, parental money behaviors become our early rulebook. Unless we consciously rewrite those rules, they continue to shape how we earn, spend, and share. What looks like personal choice is often generational financial patterns in disguise.

Many inherited scripts stay dormant until intimacy wakes them. When we join finances and make decisions together with a partner, we're not just taking care of present-day logistics. We're stirring up old defenses that may no longer fit who we are.

Common Triggers

Intimate relationships create the perfect conditions for financial trauma to resurface or begin to heal. Common contexts include:

- Joint financial decisions that require surrendering individual control
- Financial disclosures that expose hidden realities
- Shared goals that challenge long-held money beliefs
- Financial setbacks experienced as a couple
- Different money management styles that feel unsafe

These moments can activate the nervous system, leading to responses like growing combative, mentally "checking out," or going emotionally numb. The trouble comes when partners misread these reactions as stubbornness, irresponsibility, or apathy. That misreading adds yet another barrier to communication and cooperation.

How Financial Trauma Develops Within Relationships

Relationships can magnify what's already there: wounds or wellness, stress or stability.

Certain patterns, such as unequal power, unrealistic financial expectations, or financial abuse, can intensify strain and erode connection.

Unequal Financial Contributions

Earning different amounts isn't just a numbers game. It's a deeply personal journey of understanding each other's value, identity, and belonging. Every shared expense tells a story about who we are together. Income differences can tangle self-worth with contribution, stirring resentment, dependence, and unspoken expectations.

Case Study: Measuring Worth Beyond Dollars

Malcolm, a freelance graphic designer, and Sienna, a tenured professor, built their relationship on mutual respect. But the unpredictable rhythm of Malcolm's income began to create subtle tensions that neither could name. While Sienna's steady paycheck provided a consistent financial foundation, Malcolm's creative work ebbed and flowed, shaping an invisible imbalance between them.

The strain showed up in small, almost imperceptible ways. During months when Malcolm's freelance projects were scarce, he felt inadequate, haunted by the belief that he wasn't pulling his weight. Sienna, without meaning to, would sometimes reinforce those feelings through casual remarks about budgeting or financial planning that left Malcolm feeling exposed and dependent.

Their turning point came not through a dramatic confrontation but a moment of vulnerability. Malcolm confessed his fear that his worth depended on his income, a narrative inherited from his entrepreneurial parents who equated success with steady earnings. Sienna admitted her own impulse to control money as a way to feel secure.

Malcolm's shame wasn't just about an income gap; it was trauma. His body reacted to Sienna's well-meant comments with the same alarm he'd felt as a child during his parents' financial struggles.

Working with a financial therapist, they reframed what *contribution* meant. Together, they began valuing Malcolm's creative energy not only in dollars but also in the texture of their shared life. His design work brought beauty and style to their home, his flexible schedule allowed for family care, and his creative spirit nourished their relationship in ways that money couldn't measure.

Over time, Sienna and Malcolm transformed their financial story from a source of vague tension into a foundation for mutual respect. They built a more holistic framework, one that honored both material and intangible contributions. In doing so, they found a deeper intimacy that celebrated their individual strengths while creating a truly collaborative financial narrative. Their story reminds us that healing is possible when financial pain is named and held with compassion.

Unrealistic Expectations

For some, the tension isn't about how much is earned but how much is expected.

Money expectations often grow from cultural scripts, family history, or private dreams. Left unspoken, they can ignite conflict.

Ella grew up believing success meant owning a home by thirty. Sam, shaped by a more precarious past, prized freedom from debt above all else. Their shared future became a battleground of competing money meanings.

For Ella and Sam to move forward, they'll need the kind of trauma-aware communication explored later in this chapter: tools that help partners recognize when money disagreements are actually old wounds speaking.

When dreams clash with reality, the friction can uncover misaligned hopes or reveal deeper pain waiting to be addressed.

Financial Abuse

While this chapter centers on patterns of financial trauma that arise within relationships, some dynamics cross a line into abuse. When one partner uses money to isolate, control, or punish the other, the issue is no longer just about past wounds. It becomes a matter of safety. If you're navigating something that feels coercive or unsafe, know that this kind of control is called *financial abuse*.[56]

If you recognize these patterns, your priority is not reconciliation; it's protection. Safety must come first.

Managing Financial Trauma in Relationships

Money troubles are sneaky. They slip into everyday interactions: a tense talk about a surprise bill, resentment over spending habits, unease around disclosure. Small signals often point to deeper patterns. Ignoring them doesn't make them disappear; they grow, eroding trust over time.

The upside is that awareness is the first step toward healing. Naming these money patterns is like flipping on a light in a dark room. Suddenly, you can see where to go. It's not about fixing everything overnight but about moving forward with intention.

The following strategies are designed to help couples navigate financial trauma together, transforming sources of conflict into opportunities for connection and growth.

Open Communication

For many with financial trauma, money conversations feel loaded. Past experiences may have linked them with conflict or shame. Avoidance feels safer but keeps wounds alive.

Instead of diving into spreadsheets, start with feelings. Ask questions:

- "What did money mean to you growing up?"
- "What financial problems worry you the most?"
- "When I talk about money, what do you notice in your body?"

The goal isn't to solve everything at once, but to build trust through curiosity and empathy.

Shared Financial Planning

Approach planning as collaboration, not control. Begin at an easy pace. Set one goal together, celebrate small wins, and acknowledge past struggles. Each step shifts the focus from fear to empowerment and turns planning into partnership.

Professional Help

Sometimes wounds feel too tangled to untie alone. Professional help can provide a neutral, compassionate space to work through trauma, practice healthy communication, and guide conversations that feel too charged to handle solo. Seeking this kind of support is a personal choice, but it isn't admitting defeat. It signals your dedication to healing and to each other.

Recognizing Trauma Responses in the Moment

Awareness is the foundation. You can't regulate what you don't recognize.

Notice your own patterns:

- "My chest tightens during money talks."
- "I catch myself wanting to change the subject."
- "My thoughts are racing and I can't focus on what you're saying."

Partner Awareness

Trauma-aware communication between partners has two layers:

The first is ongoing, general communication. Have ongoing conversations about each other's predictable patterns. For example:

- "When you see me start to shut down, that's usually my freeze response."
- "If I start talking fast about budgets, I'm probably anxious."
- "Here's what helps me when you notice I'm getting overwhelmed."

The second is in-the-moment communication. This involves real-time recognition and gentle intervention. For example:

- "I notice your hands are clenched. Want to pause?"
- "I think I'm activated. Can we take a break?"
- "Your voice just changed. What's going on for you?"

The aim is to become a trauma-aware team, able to notice activation in yourselves and each other and to address it without shame or judgment. This approach makes the invisible visible and gives you and your partner practical tools for navigating the inevitable bumps in your financial journey.

When Conversations Go Off Track

Even with the best intentions, money talks derail. That's normal. Here's a reset process you can try:

1. Pause without blame.
2. Regulate your nervous system: breathe, ground, step outdoors.
3. Repair the connection with empathy.
4. Address underlying needs and boundaries.

What Progress Looks Like

Healing isn't linear, but progress leaves markers. Journal prompts can help you track movement:

- How does my body feel during money talks?
- What topics do I avoid, and why?
- When do I feel most and least safe discussing money?

For Jon and Mateo, progress meant setting aside twenty minutes each Sunday to talk about finances without distractions. At first, the conversations felt a little awkward as they learned each other's predictable patterns and experimented with ways to express concerns in real time. But after a few months, their money talks began to feel less like budget reviews and more like shared check-ins about hopes and concerns.

Everyone's process is unique. The key is to notice forward movement, no matter the amount, and honor it.

Continue your exploration with the questions below:

Reflection Questions

How did my family's approach to money shape the way I communicate about finances today?

Am I aware of my partner's potential trauma responses?

When have I felt a strong emotional reaction during a financial conversation with my partner? What might have been beneath that reaction?

What's one financial habit or conversation I could approach differently to create more safety and trust in my relationship?

Moving Forward

Financial trauma in relationships is complex but manageable. Healing requires trust and new neural pathways built through safe financial experiences over time. When partners notice how their trauma responses get activated, they can create strategies that meet both practical money needs and deeper emotional ones.

This dual focus transforms money talks from a trigger for renewed pain into an opportunity for co-regulation and healing.

By tracing the roots of financial trauma, recognizing how it shows up in daily interactions, and committing to the work of healing together, couples can transform financial conflict into deeper connection, mutual understanding, and shared growth. The process begins with small, intentional actions and the belief that those actions matter.

Wherever you and your partner are starting, know this: Growth is within reach.

Key Takeaways

- Money conflicts often activate trauma responses such as avoidance or hypervigilance, patterns explored in Chapter 2.
- Financial trauma runs deep in relationships, showing up as conflict, power struggles, or emotional withdrawal rooted in old wounds.
- Generational money patterns shape relationship behaviors. Inherited money scripts influence how partners handle finances as adults, sometimes repeating cycles of stress.
- Healing requires consistency and safety in financial interactions, helping the nervous system learn that vulnerability no longer equals danger.
- Honest conversations about fears and goals help couples address hidden trauma and create shared strategies for moving forward.

While some money wounds surface in our closest relationships, others live inside us, especially when we've "escaped" struggles our loved ones still face, creating a different kind of relational burden: one of guilt. The next chapter explores the weight of financial survivor's guilt and the tension between compassion for others and care for yourself.

11

Financial Trauma and Survivor's Guilt

Maria stares at her bank account on payday, her cursor hovering over the transfer button. Her emergency fund is finally approaching three months of expenses, something she never imagined possible growing up in a household where utilities were constantly at risk of disconnection.

But her younger sister just called about falling behind on a loan payment again, and their mom's medication costs keep rising. Maria is close to her family and wants to help, making the guilt even more complicated.

Her therapist has been helping her set financial boundaries and celebrate each step toward stability. Yet every time she succeeds in building security for herself, the guilt crashes in: *How can I have savings when my family is still struggling? Who am I to have a safety net when they're still walking the tightrope without one?*

These feelings of guilt and conflict around financial success are so common they have a name: *financial survivor's guilt.*

What You'll Learn in This Chapter

- How financial trauma, family dynamics, and cultural expectations create the foundation for survivor's guilt
- How achieving financial stability while others struggle can trigger intense guilt, self-sabotage, and relationship strain, and why this response is both common and manageable
- The four core manifestations of financial survivor's guilt: **over-giving** (becoming your family's unofficial bank), **hiding success** (downplaying achievements to stay "relatable"), **self-sabotaging** (maintaining unnecessary financial stress), and **self-questioning** (feeling lingering doubt after severing harmful dynamics)
- How to transform over-giving into sustainable support, move from hiding success to authentic integration, and develop financial self-trust without abandoning your safe connections
- How to honor both your growth and your well-being, whether that means creating sustainable boundaries or choosing protective distance from toxic patterns

Like Maria, I've stood at this crossroads. My own experience with financial survivor's guilt taught me that success after traumatic events can feel like climbing out of a pit only to find yourself holding a rope. You're torn between pulling others up and protecting yourself from being dragged back down. That tension lies at the heart of survivor's guilt.

To navigate these conflicts, we first need to explore what financial survivor's guilt is and how it shows up in daily life.

What Is Financial Survivor's Guilt?

Survivor's guilt arises when you escape a loss others still endure. It's not a formal diagnosis but a recognized symptom that can accompany PTSD or appear on its own. While the phrase *financial survivor's guilt* doesn't appear in diagnostic manuals, it captures a genuine emotional struggle, one that echoes themes in the literature on survivor guilt's and the psychological burdens of affluence.[57]

Financial survivor's guilt emerges when you reach stability while your family, friends, or community continue to struggle. It often strikes hardest for those who've escaped poverty, instability, or family dysfunction. Their steps toward security can be shadowed by persistent feelings of unworthiness or betrayal.

This chapter focuses on navigating guilt when you want to maintain connections and financial stability. But it's important to name something upfront: Not everyone feels a pull to stay connected. If your success required leaving harmful or abusive dynamics, you may rightly feel relief rather than guilt, and protecting that distance may be vital for your safety and healing.

If that's your experience, some parts of this chapter may not reflect your journey, and that's completely okay. Your path is different, and equally valid.

If you've chosen distance and still struggle with guilt, know this: Guilt after cutting ties doesn't mean you made the wrong choice. It means you're human. The question isn't whether you feel guilty but whether maintaining your boundaries serves your healing. Sometimes the most loving thing you can do, for everyone involved, is to stay away.

While financial survivor's guilt is common, it shows up differently for each person. For Maria, survivor's guilt manifests as constant anxiety about her emergency fund. For others, it creates pressure to become their family's unofficial bank or hide a job promotion. Recognizing these patterns helps us see when guilt, not rational choice, is steering our financial behavior.

Let's look at how survivor's guilt plays out in real life.

Core Manifestations of Financial Survivor's Guilt

When Nina received her first corporate bonus, she divided it among family members' bills, leaving nothing for her own debt repayment. This pattern of **over-giving** is one face of financial survivor's guilt. Those who achieve stability become their family's private emergency fund, saying yes to every request, feeling solely responsible for solving crises. Generosity itself isn't the problem; it becomes an issue when giving slips into enabling, trapping everyone in cycles without an end.

Others avoid or **hide success**. They may cling to lower-level jobs to stay "relatable." Or they may withhold news of promotions, raises, or bonuses in conversations with family. It's like maintaining two wardrobes: professional achievement for work and practiced scarcity for family.

Perhaps the most insidious pattern is **self-sabotage**. This could look like carrying unnecessary debt because "everyone else has debt." Or avoiding investments because no one in the family invests. Or maintaining paycheck-to-paycheck living, even when saving is possible, because stability feels "not like us." This self-sabotage often masquerades as virtue: *I don't want to be one of those people who care too much about money. I need to stay humble.* But in reality, it keeps you in struggle because stability feels disloyal.

A final manifestation appears for those who've chosen distance from harmful relationships: **haunting guilt**. Even years after cutting ties, success can trigger painful questions: *What if they really needed me? Am I selfish for protecting myself? Would a better person have found a way to help?* This guilt doesn't come from active requests. It comes from their absence and the unknown or vaguely known consequences of choosing safety.

The very steps that created safety can become sources of crushing guilt. They operate unconsciously, disguised as duty, humility, or family loyalty. Their roots run deep into personal histories, family systems, and cultural forces. Yet, even here, light breaks through: Awareness of these patterns and their origins helps reclaim agency.

Root Causes: Why Financial Survivor's Guilt Runs So Deep

These patterns don't develop in isolation. Financial survivor's guilt grows at the intersection of family trauma, cultural expectations, and systemic pressures.

Family dynamics often lie at the core, especially when your financial stability came through distancing yourself from harmful situations. When you achieve what parents couldn't or wouldn't—through therapy, education, relocation, or boundaries—guilt entangles with grief, anger, and loss. The trauma responses that helped you survive don't switch off with a stable paycheck. You may still wait for security to disappear or feel anxious about having "too much."

Cultural context shapes both the experience and the path forward. In collectivist cultures, where group well-being takes priority, financial success comes with expectations about giving back and sharing responsibility. Helping isn't rooted in guilt alone. It's also based on honor and social harmony. Yet balancing personal healing with group obligations takes an emotional toll. Even in individualist cultures, family loyalty and unspoken obligations create similar tensions. Many of us straddle multiple cultural identities, complicating the balance further.

Systemic forces amplify these struggles. Those who are the first in their family to break out of poverty may be expected to serve as the safety net for everyone else. Children of immigrants may wrestle with guilt over having advantages their parents sacrificed to provide. Anyone from a marginalized community may feel that personal success comes at the cost of abandoning their group in some way.

Financial survivor's guilt isn't just personal. It's relational, cultural, and structural. The good news is that there are ways to resolve a lot of this tension. It's possible to find balance: staying connected to others while remaining true to ourselves. To get there, we first need to explore how guilt complicates recovery from financial trauma.

When Guilt Derails Progress

When Jamie first started therapy for financial trauma, her progress came quickly. She opened a savings account, began tracking expenses, and negotiated a raise. Then her brother lost his job. Again.

"I derailed," she says. "All my new financial habits felt selfish. I emptied my savings to help him, then stopped therapy because I felt guilty spending money on myself while he was struggling."

But it also crossed Jamie's mind whether maintaining contact with her brother was helping either of them.

Jamie's experience reveals a painful paradox: The very tools that support recovery from financial trauma—therapy, financial planning, and career advancement—can trigger intense guilt. That guilt then undermines healing in three ways.

Guilt dismantles safety. The nervous system responses that characterize financial trauma (see Chapter 2) require stability to heal. Yet survivor's guilt compels us to dismantle that stability as soon as we build it. Security feels unbearable when others lack it, so we keep ourselves in crisis mode, maintain debt, or avoid planning altogether.

Guilt strains growth. "I decided not to tell my best friend about my promotion," says Mira, who grew up in poverty. "She's still struggling the way we did, and I couldn't handle feeling like I'd abandoned our shared experience." Financial stability in a struggling family or peer group can feel like being the only one carrying an umbrella in a rainstorm: sheltered, yet acutely aware of everyone else getting wet. To avoid that discomfort, many shrink themselves professionally, sabotage opportunities, or stay in underpaid roles.

Guilt reactivates shame. Every step toward healing prompts painful questions: *Why did I escape when others didn't? Am I betraying my family? Who am I to have these good things?* These thoughts echo old shame messages about money, worth, and belonging. Financial survivor's guilt doesn't just create new struggles. It reopens old wounds.

Healing means more than learning new money skills. It means growing in ways that still keep you connected to those you care for, if you choose, or letting go of a harmful situation with intention.

Breaking Free from Financial Survivor's Guilt

Financial survivor's guilt whispers that success is selfish.

"The first time I kept my bonus for myself," says Desmond, a software developer whose family lost their home when he was a child, "I had panic attacks for a week. But my therapist helped me see that having a healthy emergency fund meant I could help my family more sustainably in true emergencies."

Desmond's story reveals an essential truth: Healing doesn't mean abandoning your ability to help others. It means redefining it.

From Over-Giving to Intentional Support

Tania, a nurse with a sister struggling with addiction, describes her turning point:

"I realized I could either drain my savings helping my sister through repeated emergencies, or I could maintain my stability and be there for my nieces in the long run. It wasn't about choosing money over family. It was about choosing sustainable support over enabling."

Her shift illustrates what intentional giving looks like in practice. Instead of responding to every crisis, she:

- Built her own emergency fund first, creating genuine capacity to stay afloat so that she could help others
- Focused on funding her nieces' needs (school supplies, activities) rather than supporting her sister's lifestyle

- Set an annual limit for financial help and stuck to it, even when guilt surged
- Offered her time and guidance freely, while protecting her financial boundaries

This approach prioritizes building others' capacity over providing quick fixes. Knowledge outlasts cash. Presence and guidance often matter more than money.

When you *do* give financially, you could decide in advance what types of requests align with your values and limits, before emotions cloud judgment.

It's also important to recognize when guilt is being manipulated. This might look like suspicious timing (requests arriving right after you share good money news), emotional blackmail ("If you really cared..." or "Success has changed you"), and repeated crises with no learning in between.

There's a difference between support that builds capacity (education, therapy, or job training) and support that only postpones consequences. If a request feels "off," your inner wisdom may be speaking.

From Hiding Success to Authentic Integration

Hindering or downplaying your financial growth may feel like loyalty, but it fractures your identity. Staying small doesn't build lasting, authentic connection.

Vega became the first in her family to own a business. For years, she avoided mentioning it at gatherings, afraid of sounding arrogant. But as she worked on her trauma recovery, she started sharing, not just about wins, but about challenges too. She talked about risk, resilience, and what she was learning. "When I stopped trying to be humble and started trying to be human, I finally connected with my family," she said.

Her approach offers a model:

- **Focusing on values, not numbers.** Share about why financial stability matters: safety, freedom, peace of mind.
- **Bridging different financial worlds through translation.** Instead of "I maxed out my Roth IRA," try "I've been learning how to make money work for me."
- **Recognizing when silence reinforces shame.** On the other hand, visibility, when handled with care, can model positive possibilities for others and break generational cycles of lack.

Authenticity isn't arrogance. It's a bridge that lets you stay rooted in who you are while growing beyond where you started.

From Self-Sabotage to Financial Self-Trust

Financial security isn't betrayal. It's self-care.

For many shaped by trauma, self-trust feels foreign. You may have learned that survival meant putting others first or keeping yourself small. In that context, stability feels selfish or even unsafe.

But protecting your financial well-being means choosing not to repeat cycles. Each time you honor your limits and follow through on intentions, you send a powerful message to yourself: *I can be trusted with stability.*

This shift often begins with small acts:

- Keeping savings intact when a sibling asks for help
- Saying no to co-signing a loan
- Investing for retirement even if no one else in your family has

These aren't just financial choices. They're identity choices. Each one becomes a vote of confidence in your future, affirming your right to be safe even when others struggle.

As Desmond reflects, "I'm learning that guarding my financial stability doesn't mean I'm disloyal to where I came from. It's a testament to everything I learned about survival, transformed into something sustainable."

Self-trust is the antidote to self-sabotage. When you trust your judgment, you stop needing to prove loyalty through sacrifice. You stop confusing struggle with virtue. And you start building a life where care for yourself and care for others can finally coexist.

Finding Your Community

One of the most healing realizations is that you're not alone.

Support takes many forms. Peer groups for first-generation professionals or adults from difficult upbringings provide powerful validation. These spaces let you voice feelings that might be misunderstood as ungrateful or selfish elsewhere.

Professional mental health support can also help you navigate the complex intersection of trauma and money by:

- Processing guilt and grief about family members who still struggle
- Building financial confidence while navigating guilt
- Creating healthy money boundaries despite trauma responses
- Handling ongoing requests from family or old friends

Integration: Dancing with Two Rhythms

Healing from survivor's guilt can mean dancing to two rhythms at once: moving forward while feeling a pull toward the past. The path forward doesn't mean becoming hardened or detached. It means building a relationship with money that honors both your past and your present needs: acknowledging the strength it took to survive, while recognizing what you need now.

If you're still connected to those who struggle, you may feel like you're holding the rope for those left in the pit. But now, you know how to manage it: choosing when and how to pull, without being dragged back down. And if you've let go of that rope entirely to protect yourself, you're learning that your hands are free to build something new.

Reflection Questions

When do you feel most pulled to give from guilt rather than from choice?

What boundaries could help you support others without sacrificing your own stability?

In what ways are you still hiding your financial growth, and what would it mean to show up more fully?

Key Takeaways

- Survivor's guilt is an understandable response when achieving stability after financial trauma.
- While generosity is valuable, giving driven by guilt can enable harmful patterns and undermine long-term well-being for both giver and receiver.
- Boundaries don't necessarily mean abandonment. They can create sustainable ways to care for both yourself and your loved ones.
- Building security while managing survivor's guilt is possible with self-kindness, self-trust, clear boundaries, and ongoing support.

In the next chapter, we'll shift from healing the past to celebrating progress and preparing for what comes next. You've done the deep work. Now it's time to reflect, integrate, and step into the next phase of your healing.

12

Carrying This Forward

You've reached the last chapter. You've done hard, emotional work. Now you get to reflect on how far you've come and what it means to carry this new awareness into your everyday life.

Before we look ahead, let's pause for a moment.

You've just walked through some of the most vulnerable territory a person can explore: your relationship with money—shaped by the past, often hidden from view, influencing how you move through life.

And maybe now, you're wondering: What's next?

Let's not rush to the answer. Let's stay here for just a beat longer. Because before we move forward, something important needs to happen.

We need to name what you've done.

You've started asking questions most people avoid. *Why does money feel so charged? Why do I react the way I do? Why do I keep repeating patterns that don't serve me?* You didn't just skim the surface. You looked back into your upbringing, your identity, your past experiences, and you faced truths that might have been buried for years.

And somewhere along the way, you began to see something clearly: Your financial struggles weren't just about numbers. They were about wounds. About messages you absorbed, systems you endured, and moments that left a mark.

It's possible no one ever told you this before, so let's say it plainly now: What happened to you matters. Your reactions make sense.

Your Experience Is Real, Even If Others Don't Understand It

There's no universal scale for trauma. Some wounds come from childhood. Others arrive later, through loss, upheaval, discrimination, or fear. Some are loud. Others whisper for decades before we recognize them.

So if part of you still questions whether your pain "counts," know this: Your nervous system doesn't lie. The tension, the avoidance, the spiral of panic after spending money on yourself: those are real. Your body remembers, even if your mind tries to minimize it.

But now? You remember too. And that changes everything.

This Work Is Not to Fix but First to Understand

A lot of people approach their money challenges with the goal to "get it together." Earn more. Budget better. Be responsible, disciplined, and in control. This perspective treats money management as a simple matter of competence or effort.

But you've seen the deeper truth. You can't build a healthy financial future on top of unexamined pain. You can't shame yourself into change. You can't hustle your way out of trauma.

What *you* have done is something far more radical and effective.

You've chosen to start with acceptance. To notice patterns instead of blaming yourself for them. To view your reactions as valid data about your own experience. To make space for self-compassion instead of judgment. This is the pivot point where transformation begins.

Carl Rogers said, "The curious paradox is that when I accept myself just as I am, then I can change." By accepting your current self, you remove the resistance and pressure that hinder genuine growth, creating the psychological safety and clarity needed to move forward.

True, lasting transformation then becomes less about forceful striving and more about nurturing your authentic needs. And that's the essence of this work: not quick fixes, but safety and self-acceptance.

What Progress Really Looks Like

Maybe you didn't overhaul your finances while reading this book. That was never the expectation. Progress here has a different meaning.

It's noticing that familiar tightening in your chest before opening a bill and choosing not to run. It's pausing after the urge to overspend and asking, *what am I really needing right now?* It's choosing curiosity over self-criticism, even once.

As you move forward, you might find yourself naturally doing things differently. Having a money conversation you've avoided. Opening that long-ignored financial statement. Recognizing a shame spiral before it takes over and meeting it with compassion instead. Setting a boundary with a family member. Simply noticing a trigger without reacting to it.

Those moments matter more than you may think. Every conscious decision, every deep breath you take instead of reacting on autopilot, is a step toward lasting financial well-being and peace.

These aren't assignments. They're invitations. Trust yourself to know what feels right next.

A New Beginning

Somewhere between the first page and this one, you made a choice. You chose to look at the parts of your financial life that hurt. You chose to question the stories you've been telling yourself. You chose to stay, even when it would have been easier to close the book and walk away.

And because you've had the courage to do this work, here's the profound shift: You've built a new foundation. You've stopped fighting yourself and adding self-judgment on top of the pain. You've started responding to your financial life from a place of understanding rather than fear.

This new perspective is your bedrock. Everything you build from here will rest on it: every boundary you set, every conversation you have, every financial decision you make. And unlike the shaky ground of willpower and forced discipline, this foundation won't crumble when life gets hard. It's built on the solid ground of self-knowledge.

The work doesn't end here, of course. There will be moments when old patterns resurface, when panic floods your system, when you wonder if anything has really changed. In those moments, you'll have what you didn't have before: the preparation to meet them. You now possess skills, tools, practices, and above all, awareness. The ability to pause. The knowledge that your reaction makes sense. The compassion to meet yourself where you are.

That's not nothing. That's everything.

So as you close this book, know this: You're not the same person who opened it. You've done the hard work of understanding. You've granted yourself the grace to heal at your own pace. You've taken the first essential steps on a journey that will continue to unfold in ways you can't yet imagine.

The path forward is yours to walk. You are ready.

Acknowledgments

I'm grateful to the generous readers who previewed this book and shared their thoughtful reflections along the way. Their encouragement helped me trust the heart of this work, and their insights made it stronger. Thank you for giving your time, your attention, and your honesty.

Kate King, LPC
David R. Kopacz, MD
Ron Manderscheid, PhD
Bobby Newell, LCSW
Omar Reda, MD

Endnotes

1 Substance Abuse and Mental Health Services Administration, Practical Guide for Implementing a Trauma-Informed Approach, SAMHSA Publication No. PEP23-06-05-005 (Rockville, MD: National Mental Health and Substance Use Policy Laboratory, Substance Abuse and Mental Health Services Administration, 2023).

2 Ellie Violet Bramley, "The trauma doctor: Gabor Maté on happiness, hope and how to heal our deepest wounds," The Guardian (U.S.), April 12, 2023, https://www.theguardian.com/lifeandstyle/2023/apr/12/the-trauma-doctor-gabor-mate-on-happiness-hope-and-how-to-heal-our-deepest-wounds

3 Diagnostic and Statistical Manual of Mental Disorders: DSM-5-TR. Washington, DC: American Psychiatric Association Publishing, 2022; Amanda Ann Gregory, "Why Not All Trauma Leads to PTSD: PTSD Always Involves Trauma, but Trauma Doesn't Always Involve PTSD," Psychology Today, January 24, 2023, https://www.psychologytoday.com/us/blog/simplifying-complex-trauma/202301/why-not-all-trauma-leads-to-ptsd

4 Experian. (2023, October 25). New research reveals over two-thirds of adults have experienced financial trauma [Press release]. https://www.experianplc.com/media/latest-news/2023/financial-trauma-survey

5 American Psychological Association. (2024, October 21). Stress in America 2024: A nation in political turmoil. American Psychological Association.

6 Ogle, C. M., Rubin, D. C., & Siegler, I. C. (2014). Cumulative exposure to traumatic events in older adults. Aging & Mental Health, 18(3), 316-325.

7 Van der Kolk, B. A. (2014). The Body Keeps the Score: Brain, Mind, and Body in the Healing of Trauma

8 Ross III, D. Bruce, and Ed Coambs. "The impact of psychological trauma on finance: Narrative financial therapy considerations in exploring complex trauma and impaired financial decision making." Journal of Financial Therapy 9, no. 2 (2018): 4.

9 Bremner, J. Douglas. "Traumatic stress: effects on the brain." Dialogues in clinical neuroscience 8, no. 4 (2006): 445-461.

10 Shin, Lisa M., Scott L. Rauch, and Roger K. Pitman. "Amygdala, medial prefrontal cortex, and hippocampal function in PTSD." Annals of the New York Academy of Sciences 1071, no. 1 (2006): 67-79.

11 Mobbs, Dean, Cindy C. Hagan, Tim Dalgleish, Brian Silston, and Charlotte Prévost. "The ecology of human fear: survival optimization and the nervous system." Frontiers in neuroscience 9 (2015): 121062.

12 Porges, Stephen W. The polyvagal theory: Neurophysiological foundations of emotions, attachment, communication, and self-regulation (Norton series on interpersonal neurobiology). WW Norton & Company, 2011.

13 Hanson, Rick. Hardwiring happiness: The new brain science of contentment, calm, and confidence. Harmony, 2013.

14 Gee, Dylan G., Laurel J. Gabard-Durnam, Jessica Flannery, Bonnie Goff, Kathryn L. Humphreys, Eva H. Telzer, Todd A. Hare, Susan Y. Bookheimer, and Nim Tottenham. "Early developmental emergence of human amygdala–prefrontal connectivity after maternal deprivation." Proceedings of the National Academy of Sciences 110, no. 39 (2013): 15638-15643.

15 Piaget, Jean. The child's conception of the world: Transl. by Joan and Andrew Tomlinson. Paladin, 1973.

16 Klontz, Bradley, Sonya L. Britt, Jennifer Mentzer, and Ted Klontz. "Money beliefs and financial behaviors: Development of the Klontz Money Script Inventory." Journal of Financial Therapy 2, no. 1 (2011): 1.

17 Experian. (2023, October 25). New research reveals over two-thirds of adults have experienced financial trauma [Press release]. https://www.experianplc.com/media/latest-news/2023/financial-trauma-survey

18 Richardson, Safiya, Jonathan A. Shaffer, Louise Falzon, David Krupka, Karina W. Davidson, and Donald Edmondson. "Meta-analysis of perceived stress and its association with incident coronary heart disease." The American journal of cardiology 110, no. 12 (2012): 1711-1716; Tian, Fan, Qing Shen, Yihan Hu, Weimin Ye, Unnur A. Valdimarsdottir, Huan Song, and Fang Fang. "Association of stress-related disorders with subsequent risk of all-cause and cause-specific mortality: A population-based and sibling-controlled cohort study." The Lancet Regional Health–Europe 18 (2022); Davis, Margaret T., Sophie E. Holmes, Robert H. Pietrzak, and Irina Esterlis. "Neurobiology of chronic stress-related psychiatric disorders: evidence from molecular imaging studies." Chronic Stress1 (2017): 2470547017710916; Mariotti, Agnese. "The effects of chronic stress on health: new insights into the molecular mechanisms of brain–body communication." Future science OA 1, no. 3 (2015): FSO23.

19 Discover® and Thrive Global, Thriving Wallet Research Insights Report (New York: Discover Financial Services and Thrive Global, 2020), "Potential Impacts on Sleep," 9, https://content.thriveglobal.com/wp-content/uploads/2020/02/Thriving-Wallet-Research-Insights-Report.pdf.

20 Cardello, Lisa M., and Galaxina G. Wright. "Infusing trauma-informed care in career counseling: Promising practices and a proposed framework." Trauma Counseling and Resilience 1, no. 1 (2024): 5.

21 Kory Floyd et al., "The Connection Prescription: Using the Power of Social Interactions for Good Health," Journal of Mental Health and Clinical Psychology (2015): 5-12, https://pmc.ncbi.nlm.nih.gov/articles/PMC6125010/.

22 Chou, Chia-Ying, Janice Y. Tsoh, Lauren C. Smith, L. David Bain, Luba Botcheva, Elena Chan, Joanne Chan et al. "How is hoarding related to trauma? A detailed examination on different aspects of hoarding and age when hoarding started." Journal of obsessive-compulsive and related disorders 16 (2018): 81-87.

23 Bhatnagar, Rishabh. "Spending in Trauma: A Study on How Trauma Impacts Spending Behavior in College Students." (2025).

24 Abate, Biruk Beletew, Ashenafi Kibret Sendekie, Abebe Merchaw, Gebremeskel Kibret Abebe, Molla Azmeraw, Addis Wondmagegn Alamaw, Alemu Birara Zemariam et al. "Adverse childhood experiences are associated with mental health problems later in life: An umbrella review of systematic review and meta-analysis." Neuropsychobiology 84, no. 1 (2025): 48-63; Caglayan, Safak, Anne Høye, Jens C. Thimm, Catharina EA Wang, and Ole K. Grønli. "Association of adverse childhood experiences with physical illness and self-rated health in the population-based Tromsø Study." European Journal of Public Health 35, no. 3 (2025): 498-504.

25 Halfon, Neal, Kandyce Larson, John Son, Michael Lu, and Christina Bethell. "Income inequality and the differential effect of adverse childhood experiences in US children." Academic pediatrics 17, no. 7 (2017): S70-S78.

26 Zhang, Xiaoyan, and Shannon M. Monnat. "Racial/ethnic differences in clusters of adverse childhood experiences and associations with adolescent mental health." SSM-population health 17 (2022): 100997; Richards, Tara N., Joseph A. Schwartz, and Emily Wright. "Examining adverse childhood experiences among Native American persons in a nationally representative sample: Differences among racial/ethnic groups and race/ethnicity-sex dyads." Child Abuse & Neglect 111 (2021): 104812.

27 Johnson, Sara B., Anne W. Riley, Douglas A. Granger, and Jenna Riis. "The science of early life toxic stress for pediatric practice and advocacy." Pediatrics 131, no. 2 (2013): 319-327.

28 Cross, Dorthie, Negar Fani, Abigail Powers, and Bekh Bradley. "Neurobiological development in the context of childhood trauma." Clinical psychology: science and practice 24, no. 2 (2017): 111.

29 Knifton, Lee, and Greig Inglis. "Poverty and mental health: policy, practice and research implications." BJPsych bulletin 44, no. 5 (2020): 193-196.

30 Rashmi Chimmalgi and Meghan Kissellk, The Not-So-Simple Truth about the Gender Pay Gap: 2025 Update (American Association of University Women (AAUW), February 2025), 3.

31 Beccia, Ariel L., S. Bryn Austin, Jonggyu Baek, Madina Agénor, Sarah Forrester, Eric Y. Ding, William M. Jesdale, and Kate L. Lapane. "Cumulative exposure to state-level structural sexism and risk of disordered eating: results from a 20-year prospective cohort study." Social Science & Medicine 301 (2022): 114956.

32 Covey, S. R. (1989). The 7 Habits of Highly Effective People: Restoring the Character Ethic. New York: Free Press.

33Stephen J. McNamee and Robert K. Miller, The Meritocracy Myth, 5th ed. (Lanham, MD: Rowman & Littlefield, 2024); Drissen, Yvette. "Ashamed of Being Poor: The Merciless Belief in Meritocracy." In The Moral Psychology of Poverty. 2025.

34 Experian, New research, n. 4.

35 Gladstone, Joe J., Jon M. Jachimowicz, Adam Eric Greenberg, and Adam D. Galinsky. "Financial shame spirals: How shame intensifies financial hardship." Organizational Behavior and Human Decision Processes 167 (2021): 42-56.

36 Budiarto, Yohanes, and Avin Fadilla Helmi. "Shame and self-esteem: A meta-analysis." Europe's journal of psychology 17, no. 2 (2021): 131.

37 Fine, Naomi B., Ziv Ben-Zion, Iftah Biran, and Talma Hendler. "Neuroscientific account of Guilt-and Shame-Driven PTSD phenotypes." European Journal of Psychotraumatology 14, no. 2 (2023): 2202060.

38 Dolezal, Luna, and Barry Lyons. "Health-related shame: an affective determinant of health?" Medical humanities 43, no. 4 (2017): 257-263.

39 Wilson, J. P., Droždek, B., & Turkovic, S. (2006). Posttraumatic shame and guilt. Trauma, Violence, & Abuse, 7(2), 122-141.

40 Plante, Wendy, Lea Tufford, and Tanya Shute. "Interventions with survivors of interpersonal trauma: addressing the role of shame." Clinical social work journal 50, no. 2 (2022): 183-193.

41 Wulff, J. M., & Wulff, M. S. H. (2017, June 1). The neurobiology of traumatic stress: An overview of the current literature on brain changes, deficits in executive function, and impulsivity. Journal of Psychosocial Nursing and Mental Health Services, 55(6), 25–30.

42 Rankin, Howard J. "The Psychological Dangers of Marketing: The Psychological Impact of Marketing Manipulation and Extremist Messaging." How Not to Think, Psychology Today, June 26, 2024. https://www.psychologytoday.com/us/blog/how-not-to-think/202406/the-psychological-dangers-of-marketing

43 Boyraz, Güler, J. Brandon Waits, Victoria A. Felix, and Danita D. Wynes. "Posttraumatic stress and physical health among adults: The role of coping mechanisms." Journal of loss and trauma 21, no. 1 (2016): 47-61.

44 Richardson, Thomas, Peter Elliott, and Ronald Roberts. "The relationship between personal unsecured debt and mental and physical health: a systematic review and meta-analysis." Clinical psychology review 33, no. 8 (2013): 1148-1162; Richardson, Safiya, Jonathan A. Shaffer, Louise Falzon, David Krupka, Karina W. Davidson, and Donald Edmondson. "Meta-analysis of perceived stress and its association with incident coronary heart disease." The American journal of cardiology 110, no. 12 (2012): 1711-1716; Tian, Fan, Qing Shen, Yihan Hu, Weimin Ye, Unnur A. Valdimarsdottir, Huan Song, and Fang Fang. "Association of stress-related disorders with subsequent risk of all-cause and cause-specific mortality: A population-based and sibling-controlled cohort study." The Lancet Regional Health–Europe 18 (2022).

45 Discover® and Thrive Global, Thriving Wallet Research Insights Report (New York: Discover Financial Services and Thrive Global, 2020), "Potential

Impacts on Sleep," 9, https://content.thriveglobal.com/wp-content/uploads/2020/02/Thriving-Wallet-Research-Insights-Report.pdf.

46 Arnsten, Amy FT. "Stress signalling pathways that impair prefrontal cortex structure and function." Nature reviews neuroscience 10, no. 6 (2009): 410-422.

47 Fisher, Janina. Healing the fragmented selves of trauma survivors: Overcoming internal self-alienation. Routledge, 2017.

48 Siegel, Daniel J. The developing mind: How relationships and the brain interact to shape who we are. Guilford Publications, 2020.

49 Bessel A. Van der Kolk, The Body Keeps the Score: Brain, Mind, and Body in the Healing of Trauma. Penguin Books, 2014.

50 Putica, Andrea, and James Agathos. "Reconceptualizing complex posttraumatic stress disorder: a predictive processing framework for mechanisms and intervention." Neuroscience & Biobehavioral Reviews 164 (2024): 105836.

51 Gillespie, Lane. "Survey: 43% of Americans say money is negatively impacting their mental health." Bankrate. April 30, 2025. https://www.bankrate.com/banking/money-and-mental-health-survey/.

52 Jiménez-Solomon, Oscar, Irwin Garfinkel, Melanie Wall, and Christopher Wimer. "When money and mental health problems pile up: The reciprocal relationship between income and psychological distress." SSM-Population Health 25 (2024): 101624.

53 Guan, Naijie, Alessandra Guariglia, Patrick Moore, Fangzhou Xu, and Hareth Al-Janabi. "Financial stress and depression in adults: A systematic review." PloS one 17, no. 2 (2022): e0264041.

54 "Financial Distress & the Family," American Association for Marriage and Family Therapy, accessed October 28, 2025, https://www.aamft.org/AAMFT/Consumer_Updates/Financial_Distress.aspx#:~:text=Mental%20health%20

issues%2C%20such%20as,financial%20strain%20effects%20on%20
relationships

55 Turunen, Elina, and Heikki Hiilamo. "Health effects of indebtedness: a systematic review." BMC public health 14, no. 1 (2014): 489.

56 Sharp-Jeffs, Nicola. "A review of research and policy on financial abuse within intimate partner relationships." (2015).

57 Hannah Murray, "Survivor Guilt: A Cognitive Approach," Frontiers in Psychology 12 (2021): 1–11; Suniya S. Luthar, "The Culture of Affluence: Psychological Costs of Material Wealth," Child Development 74, no. 6 (2003): 1581–1593.

Index

A

B

C

D

E

F

G

H

I

M

N

O

P

R

S

T

W

About the Author

Wendy Molyneux, MSW, CFEI®, writes and teaches about the interconnectedness of money and all areas of life.

A social worker by training and a financial well-being advocate by calling, she draws on both lived experience and years of professional practice to help people understand and transform their relationship with money.

As founder of WholePerson.finance, Wendy encourages a compassionate, holistic, trauma-informed approach to financial wellness.

If This Book Helped You

If this book resonated with you, I'd be grateful if you'd consider sharing your experience. An honest review on Goodreads, Amazon, or wherever you purchased this book helps others discover whether it might support their own journey. Your perspective matters. It only takes a moment, but it makes a meaningful difference in connecting this work with those who need it most.

Thank you for your time and trust and for helping this book's message reach others.

Beyond These Pages

Now that you've begun this journey, you may sense there's more to uncover. For ongoing support, supplementary tools, and continued exploration in trauma-aware holistic finance, please visit WholePerson.finance.

There, you'll find additional resources designed to support the important work you've started. Take what you need, try what fits, and revisit the site whenever you're ready for the next layer of reflection.

To stay informed about future resources and to be the first to know when the next book is released, you can also sign up for updates on the website.

The Journey Continues

In the upcoming volume, we'll go deeper into the practices that help you manage and integrate financial trauma. The next book explores how to:

- Reframe limiting beliefs rooted in trauma.
- Align your money habits with your core values.
- Soothe your nervous system during financial stress (continued).
- Choose among advanced psychological, somatic, and holistic tools.
- Build resilience and foster post-traumatic growth.

That said, you don't need the next book to move forward. Everything in this volume was designed to help you begin and sustain a meaningful healing journey. You already have the tools necessary to make conscious financial choices that serve you now. The next volume is simply an invitation to do further, advanced work, should you choose to accept it.

Wherever your journey takes you next, I'm honored we walked this part together.

Made in United States
North Haven, CT
06 November 2026

21884527R00136